HOW FAR WOULD YOU GO?
FAX +44 (0)20 7407 9075
BEST RESPONSES PRINTED IN THE D&AD STUDENT AWARDS ANNUAL 2003
WWW.DANDAD.ORG

WHAT IS IT YOU REALLY WANT?
FAX +44 (0)20 7407 9075
BEST RESPONSES PRINTED IN THE D&AD STUDENT AWARDS ANNUAL 2003
WWW.DANDAD.ORG

D&AD STUDENT AWARDS 2003
CALL FOR ENTRIES

WOULD IT HELP IF YOU WERE BEAUTIFUL?
FAX +44 (0)20 7407 9075
BEST RESPONSES PRINTED IN THE D&AD STUDENT AWARDS ANNUAL 2003
WWW.DANDAD.ORG

D&AD STUDENT AWARDS 2003
CALL FOR ENTRIES

CAN YOU DRAW A FERRET?
FAX +44 (0)20 7407 9075
BEST RESPONSES PRINTED IN THE D&AD STUDENT AWARDS ANNUAL 2003
WWW.DANDAD.ORG

D&AD STUDENT AWARDS 2003
CALL FOR ENTRIES

D&AD STUDENT AWARDS 2003
THE ANNUAL

CONTENTS
002 LETTERS FROM THE EDUCATION CHAIRMAN AND EDUCATION DIRECTOR, D&AD
004 THANK YOU – ANNUAL SPONSOR

BRIEFS
006 STUDENT OF THE YEAR
010 WPP BURSARIES
014 ADVERTISING – POSTCARD MEDIA
022 ADVERTISING – TRANSPORT MEDIA
028 ADVERTISING CAMPAIGN – OPEN BRIEF
034 AMBIENT MEDIA
042 BRAND IDENTITY AND DEVELOPMENT
050 CORUS STEEL PACKAGING
064 DIRECT MAIL
072 DIRECT RESPONSE
076 ENVIRONMENTAL DESIGN
082 GRAPHIC DESIGN
088 ILLUSTRATION
094 INFORMATION DESIGN
100 INTERACTIVE DESIGN
104 MIXED MEDIA
110 NESTA PRODUCT DESIGN AND INNOVATION AWARDS
118 PHOTOGRAPHY
126 POSTER ADVERTISING
132 PRESS ADVERTISING
138 RADIO ADVERTISING
146 STREAMING
152 TV GRAPHICS
160 TV SHORT
162 TYPOGRAPHY
170 WEBSITE DESIGN
176 WRITING

184 CONTACT DETAILS
186 SUMMARY OF WINNING COLLEGES
187 INDEX OF STUDENTS
188 D&AD STUDENT AWARDS SCHEME
192 ACKNOWLEDGEMENTS

THE STUDENT ANNUAL IS SUPPORTED BY
venturaworks!

WITH SPECIAL THANKS TO
cMc

AND THANKS TO
Canon

DICK POWELL, SEYMOUR POWELL, EDUCATION CHAIRMAN, D&AD

YOU HOLD IN YOUR HANDS THE CREATIVE FUTURE OF THIS COUNTRY. WITHIN THESE PAGES YOU WILL FIND THE WORK OF THOSE MOST LIKELY TO BE TOMORROW'S STARS OF ADVERTISING AND DESIGN, FUELLING COMMERCE AND CULTURE INTO THE FUTURE.

EACH YEAR, THIS ANNUAL PROVIDES A SNAPSHOT OF THE CREATIVE ENERGY OF STUDENTS IN EVERY DESIGN DISCIPLINE ACROSS THE COUNTRY. YOUNG DESIGNERS WITH WORK IN THIS BOOK ARE MAKING THE TRANSITION FROM STUDENT TO PROFESSIONAL. IF YOUR WORK IS HERE, IT PUTS YOU A STEP ABOVE YOUR PEERS; WINNING A PENCIL, A STEP ABOVE THAT.

BUT THAT MOVE FROM STUDENT TO PROFESSIONAL INVARIABLY INVOLVES GETTING A JOB, AND THAT MEANS COMPETING, NOT JUST AGAINST YOUR FRIENDS AND PEERS, BUT ALSO ALL OF THOSE CREATIVES WHO GRADUATED THE YEAR BEFORE, AND THE YEAR BEFORE THAT. WE ALL KNOW IT'S TOUGH – TOUGHER THAN EVER, BUT BELIEVE ME, BEING IN THIS BOOK IS PROBABLY THE BEST START YOU CAN HAVE. IT GOES OUT TO THOUSANDS OF POTENTIAL EMPLOYERS AND IS WIDELY CIRCULATED IN CREATIVE DEPARTMENTS AROUND THE WORLD. DON'T FORGET, YOUR WORK HAS ALREADY BEEN JUDGED AND SELECTED BY A TEAM OF TALENTED PROFESSIONALS; YOU'RE ALREADY STARTING TO MAKE THE GRADE; YOU'RE ALREADY SETTING YOURSELF HIGH CREATIVE STANDARDS.

AND NEVER FORGET – IT'S CREATIVE STANDARDS WHICH WILL DEFINE YOUR CAREER AND VERY PROBABLY SHAPE YOUR LIFE.

Education Council

Abbott Mead Vickers.BBDO
Peter Souter

Banks Hoggins O'Shea FCB
Ken Hoggins

Bartle Bogle Hegarty
John Hegarty

BMP DDB
Chris Powell

Burkitt DDB
Jon Canning

Citigate Lloyd Northover
Jim Northover

Coley Porter Bell
Stephen Bell

Corporate Edge
Peter Shaw

Duckworth Finn Grubb Waters
Dave Waters

EHS Brann
Phil Jones

Elmwood Design
Jonathan Sands

FutureBrand
Robert Soar

Grey Worldwide
Tim Mellors

Identica
Michael Peters OBE

Interbrand
Rita Clifton

J Walter Thompson
Alistair Wood

Landor Associates
Charles Wrench

Leo Burnett
Mike McKenna

Lewis Moberly
Mary Lewis

Lowe & Partners Worldwide
Adrian Holmes

M&C Saatchi
James Lowther

Marketplace Design
Bryan Brown

Miles Calcraft Briginshaw Duffy
Paul Briginshaw

Ogilvy
Malcolm Poynton

Partners BDDH
Nick Hastings

Publicis
Gerry Moira

Rainey Kelly Campbell Roalfe/Y&R
Robert Campbell

Saatchi & Saatchi
Tony Granger

Seymour Powell
Dick Powell

Siebert Head
Keren House

St Luke's
Alan Young

Silk Pearce
Jack Pearce

TBWA\London
Trevor Beattie

The Chase
Ben Casey

The Partners
Gillian Thomas

WWAV Rapp Collins
Ian Haworth

CLAIRE FENNELOW, EDUCATION AND TRAINING DIRECTOR, D&AD

WHEN TIMES ARE TOUGH, AS THEY CURRENTLY ARE, IT IS MORE IMPORTANT THAN EVER TO STAND OUT FROM THE CROWD. ONE OF THE MOST IMPORTANT THINGS THAT D&AD CAN DO FOR A YOUNG CREATIVE IS TO GIVE THEM THAT POINT OF DIFFERENTIATION. THERE ARE SEVERAL PROGRAMMES INITIATED BY THE EDUCATION DEPARTMENT TO HELP YOU WITH THIS, BUT THE MOST EFFECTIVE METHOD IS TO WIN YOURSELF A STUDENT AWARD AND GET INTO THE STUDENT ANNUAL. THESE AWARDS ARE NOT JUST ABOUT WINNING PRIZE MONEY AND A BABY YELLOW PENCIL (ALTHOUGH WE KNOW THAT IS THE BEST BIT), BUT MAKING SURE THAT YOU GET NOTICED BY THE CREATIVE INDUSTRIES. THAT IS WHY WE INVEST SO MUCH THOUGHT, MONEY AND RESOURCE INTO THESE AWARDS, AND GUARANTEE THAT THE ANNUAL LANDS ON THE DESK OF EVERY SENIOR DESIGNER AND ADVERTISING CREATIVE. IF YOUR WORK IS IN THE BOOK, YOU WILL HAVE GAINED THAT ALL IMPORTANT DIFFERENTIATION FACTOR.

OUR MANY OTHER EDUCATION PROGRAMMES; NEW BLOOD, BLOODBANK, ADVERTISING WORKSHOPS ETC CONTINUE TO OFFER GREAT OPPORTUNITIES FOR EMERGING CREATIVES TO LEARN ABOUT THEIR CRAFT AND INDUSTRY, AND TO FINALLY SECURE THAT ALL IMPORTANT FIRST JOB BOTH HERE AND ABROAD.

NONE OF THESE ACTIVITIES WOULD BE POSSIBLE WITHOUT THE SUPPORT OF OUR SPONSORS, THE EDUCATION COUNCIL AND OF COURSE THE D&AD EDUCATION TEAM. A BIG THANK YOU TO THEM ALL FOR MAKING A DIFFERENCE.

Claire Fennelow
Education and Training Director

Jo Maude
Acting Education Director

Chris Thompson
College and Graduate Programme Manager

Anna Bailey
College Programme Manager

Ian Willingham
Student Awards Manager

Laura Woodroffe
Training Programme Manager

Nia Evans
Education Officer

ventura*works!*

ventura*honours!*

ventura*cheers!*

ventura*supports!*

ventura*inspects!*

ventura*expresses!*

ventura*bamboozles!*

ventura*passes!*

ventura*beats!*

ventura*trounces!*

ventura*prints!*

Ventura Works! Crayfields Business Park New Mill Road
St Pauls Cray Orpington Kent BR5 3QA
T 01689 887700

Gail Lingard
Glasgow School of Art

STUDENT OF THE YEAR

WRITING
CHRISTIAN STACEY
KINGSTON UNIVERSITY

JUDGES' COMMENTS WE FELT THAT THE OVERALL QUALITY OF THE SHORTLISTED ENTRIES WAS EXCELLENT. OUR FINAL DELIBERATIONS CONCERNED FIVE PIECES OF WORK BUT AFTER THOROUGH DISCUSSION, FOR ITS UTTER SIMPLICITY AND 'I WISH I'D DONE THAT' APPEAL, OUR DECISION REGARDING THE WINNER WAS UNANIMOUS. **NICK BELL**

Michael Johnson
Johnson Banks

Dick Powell
Seymour-Powell

Lynn Trickett
Trickett & Webb

Alison Tomlin
Carter Wong Tomlin

Nick Bell
J Walter Thompson

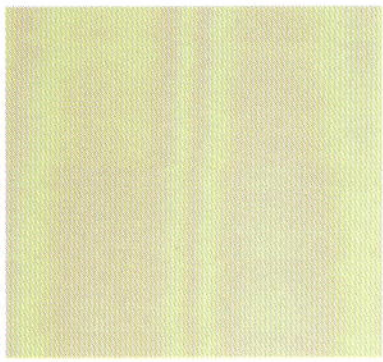

Student of the Year

Student
Christian Stacey

Tutors
Bryn Jones
Ben Tibbs
Malcolm Kennard

College
Kingston University

Term 1 Lecture Handouts

Sponsored by *The* **Guardian**

Term 1 Lecture Notice

COURSE:	ALL
MODULE:	G1 [Guardian series]
TUTOR:	Alan Rusbridger
LOCATION:	Campus Shop

KEY POINTS:

To keep up with what's going on in the world, don't discount The Guardian. We've already done that for you.

Term 1 Lecture Handout

COURSE: Psychology

MODULE: G1 [Guardian series]

TUTOR: Alan Rusbridger

LOCATION: Campus Shop

KEY POINTS:

Consider how fellow students who didn't know that they could have bought The Guardian for just 20 pence on campus, may feel when they do eventually find out. How might they react, and how will you accommodate their aggression?

Term 1 Lecture Handout

COURSE: Geography

MODULE: G1 [Guardian series]

TUTOR: Alan Rusbridger

LOCATION: Campus Shop

KEY POINTS:

Your nearest university campus shop, where The Guardian will cost you just 20p, is located at:

```
KINGSTON UNIVERSITY MINI-MART
PENRHYN ROAD
KINGSTON KT6 8EF
```

DESIGNERS
TO REALLY CONSIDER THE
IMPLICATIONS OF THEIR
DESIGN AESTHETICS.
ESPECIALLY WHEN IT
SUBSEQUENTLY CONCERNS
THE BLATANT OVER USE
OF PHOTOCOPY TONER.

WPP

WPP BURSARIES

THERE ARE FEW FORMAL GRADUATE TRAINEE PROGRAMMES FOR COLLEGE LEAVERS WHO ARE SEEKING A CAREER IN ADVERTISING OR DESIGN FIELDS. THE WPP BURSARY PROGRAMME SEEKS TO PROVIDE A VALUABLE ADDITION TO D&AD'S EXISTING ACTIVITIES, SMOOTHING THE PATH BETWEEN COLLEGE AND WORK.

OF THE 120 STUDENTS WHO APPLIED FOR THE BURSARIES, SIX ENTRANTS WERE SELECTED FOR INTERVIEW TO DETERMINE THE TWO WINNERS, EACH RECEIVING A £5,000 BURSARY AND A THREE MONTH WORK PLACEMENT AT A WPP COMPANY.

D&AD CONGRATULATE THE WINNERS OF THIS SECOND WPP BURSARY PROGRAMME.

IT GOES WITHOUT SAYING THAT THE TRANSITION FROM COLLEGE TO WORK IS DIFFICULT. THANKFULLY, THE BURSARY GAVE ME THE OPPORTUNITY TO WORK WITH LAMBIE-NAIRN, WHERE I WAS SUBSEQUENTLY TAKEN ON AS A JUNIOR DESIGNER. I COULDN'T HAVE HOPED FOR A BETTER START TO MY CAREER. **EDWARD WALKER, WPP BURSARY WINNER 2002**

WHEN WE WERE TOLD THAT WE'D GOT THROUGH, I REMEMBER JUMPING UP AND DOWN IN THE STREET… IT WASN'T JUST THE MONEY I WAS PLEASED ABOUT, IT WAS THE THOUGHT OF GETTING MY TEETH INTO DOING A LONG PLACEMENT AT OGILVY AND KNOWING WHERE I'D BE FOR THE NEXT THREE MONTHS – IT REALLY MADE A DIFFERENCE TO WHAT WE MIGHT BE DOING RIGHT NOW. **KATE PAULL AND STUART PANTOLL, WPP BURSARY WINNERS 2002**

Stephen Bell
Coley Porter Bell

Sally Nesbitt
Lambie-Nairn

Cordell Burke
OgilvyOne

Nick Parton
Ogilvy

Martin Grimer
Coley Porter Bell

Gillian Thomas
The Partners

Derek Johnston
Landor Associates

Glenn Tutssel
Tutssels
Enterprise IG

WPP Bursary Winner
Grey Ingram
(Derrick Webb also worked on this project)

Tutors
Mark Fensky
Coz Cotzias
Pat Burnham
Charlie Kouns

College
VCU Adcenter

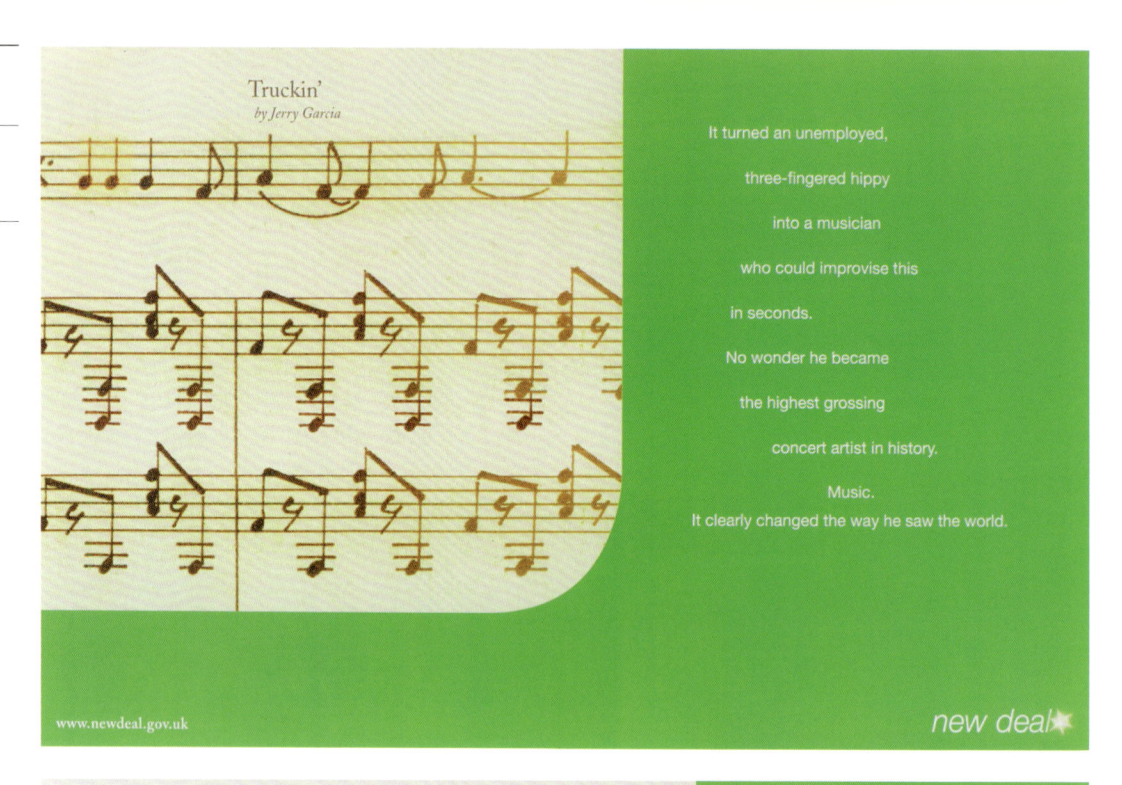

Truckin'
by Jerry Garcia

It turned an unemployed, three-fingered hippy into a musician who could improvise this in seconds. No wonder he became the highest grossing concert artist in history.

Music.
It clearly changed the way he saw the world.

www.newdeal.gov.uk

new deal

Imagine
by John Lennon

Imagine no heaven there's

Dyslexia caused him to fail out of high school. Had he not become a musician, he might be standing next to you right now.

Music.
It clearly changed the way he saw the world.

www.newdeal.gov.uk

new deal

WPP Bursary Winners
William Bingham
Victoria Daltrey

Tutors
Zelda Malan
Clive Challis
Maggie Gallagher

College
Central Saint Martins/
College of Art and Design

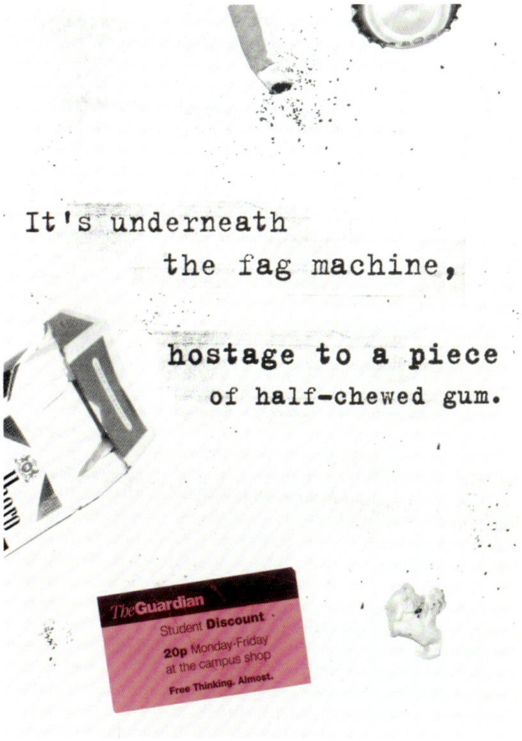

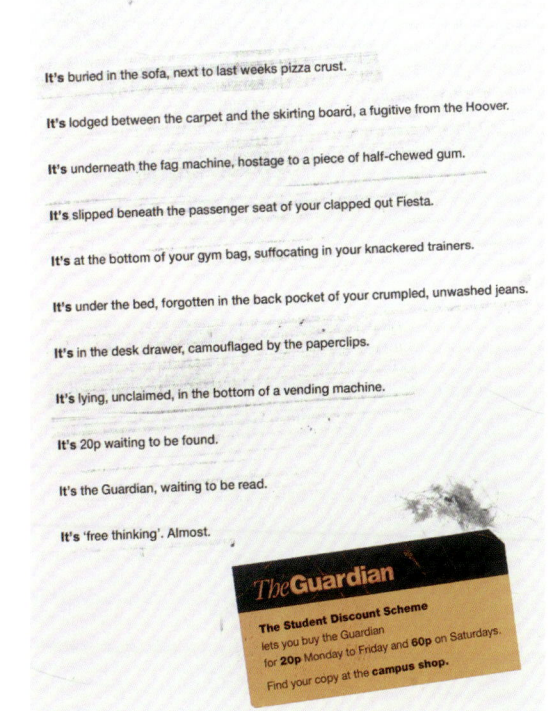

It's underneath the fag machine, hostage to a piece of half-chewed gum.

It's buried in the sofa, next to last weeks pizza crust.

It's lodged between the carpet and the skirting board, a fugitive from the Hoover.

It's underneath the fag machine, hostage to a piece of half-chewed gum.

It's slipped beneath the passenger seat of your clapped out Fiesta.

It's at the bottom of your gym bag, suffocating in your knackered trainers.

It's under the bed, forgotten in the back pocket of your crumpled, unwashed jeans.

It's in the desk drawer, camouflaged by the paperclips.

It's lying, unclaimed, in the bottom of a vending machine.

It's 20p waiting to be found.

It's the Guardian, waiting to be read.

It's 'free thinking'. Almost.

The Guardian
The Student Discount Scheme lets you buy the Guardian for **20p** Monday to Friday and **60p** on Saturdays. Find your copy at the **campus shop**.

No I can't

Draw a Ferret

Gareth Thomas
Electronics
Southampton University

boomerang

NOT FOR SALE

info@boomerangmedia.co.uk ☎ 01232 363563

D&AD STUDENT AWARDS 2003
THE BEST IN DESIGN, ADVERTISING
AND COMMUNICATIONS.

WWW.DANDAD.ORG TO DOWNLOAD
A COPY OF THE CALL FOR ENTRY BROCHURE
OR CALL +44 (0)20 7840 1113
ENTRY DEADLINE: FRIDAY 28 MARCH 2003
TOTAL PRIZE MONEY AVAILABLE: £50,000

FAX BACK THE QUESTION ON THE REVERSE
IS A BIT OF FUN. REPLIES MAY BE PUBLISHED
IN THE STUDENT AWARDS ANNUAL. FAXES MUST
INCLUDE YOUR NAME, COURSE AND COLLEGE.

Cartoon/Design by Brown's/London

SPONSORED BY BOOMERANG MEDIA

boomerang

ADVERTISING – POSTCARD MEDIA

THE BRIEF DESIGN A SERIES OF POSTCARDS ENCOURAGING YOUNG PEOPLE TO CONSIDER THE NAVY AS AN APPEALING AND VIABLE CAREER OPTION. DESIGNS SHOULD BOTH CHALLENGE MISCONCEPTIONS AND INFORM THE TARGET AUDIENCE OF THE VARIOUS CAREER OPPORTUNITIES THAT ARE AVAILABLE. THE TONE SHOULD BE UPBEAT AND ENGAGING WHILST THE MESSAGE SHOULD BE SIMPLE AND HONEST.

JUDGES' COMMENTS I WAS HOPING TO SEE A FRESH TAKE ON THE ROYAL NAVY RECRUITMENT PROPOSITION, ONE WHICH WOULD BE IN KEEPING WITH THE ATTITUDES OF THE TARGET AGE GROUP, SIMPLY BECAUSE STUDENTS FROM WITHIN THIS AGE GROUP WOULD BE WORKING ON THE BRIEF. I WANTED TO KNOW IF THEY COULD PRESENT FRESH IDEAS AND STILL MAINTAIN BRAND INTEGRITY. **SARAH CHRISTMAS**

THE MAJORITY ANSWERED ASPECTS OF THE BRIEF BUT ONLY A FEW REALLY EXPLORED IT TO PRODUCE GREAT IDEAS. NO SINGLE PIECE WORKED ON ENOUGH LEVELS OF THE BRIEF TO BE OUTSTANDING. **GARY SHARPEN**

THE COMMENDED ENTRIES WERE VERY GOOD SIMPLE IDEAS. THEY WOULD WITHOUT QUESTION MAKE ME TAKE THE CARDS OUT OF THE DISPLAY CASE! **ALEX TAYLOR**

SOME STUDENTS HAD REALLY INVESTIGATED WHAT THE ROYAL NAVY WAS ABOUT AND WHAT IT MEANT TO THE TARGET AUDIENCE. WHILE NO ONE ENTRY STOOD HEAD AND SHOULDERS ABOVE THE REST, THERE WERE A HANDFUL OF STRONG CONTENDERS. **NATHALIE WICKS**

Gary Sharpen
Leonardo

Nathalie Wicks
Boomerang Media

Sarah Christmas
Boomerang Media

Bill Wilcox
Royal Navy

Alex Taylor
Publicis

Commendation

Student
Lee Choo Chin

Tutors
Nancy Slonims
Phil Healey

College
Middlesex University

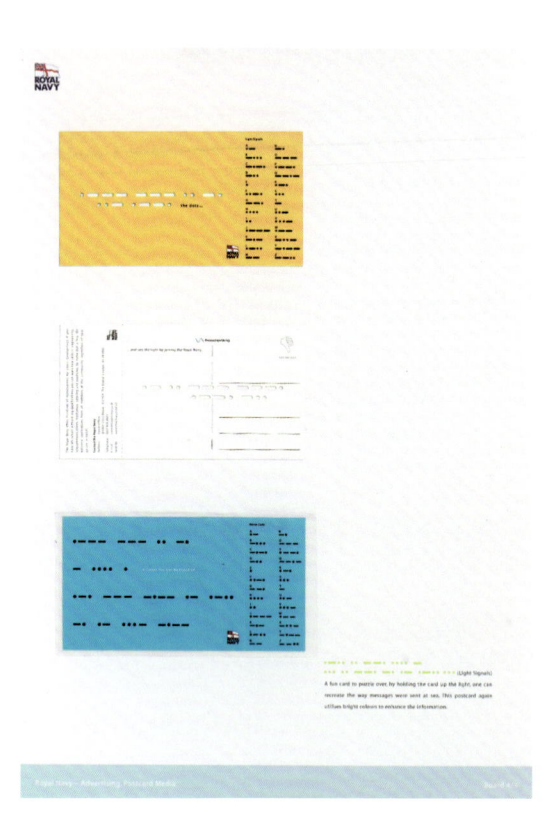

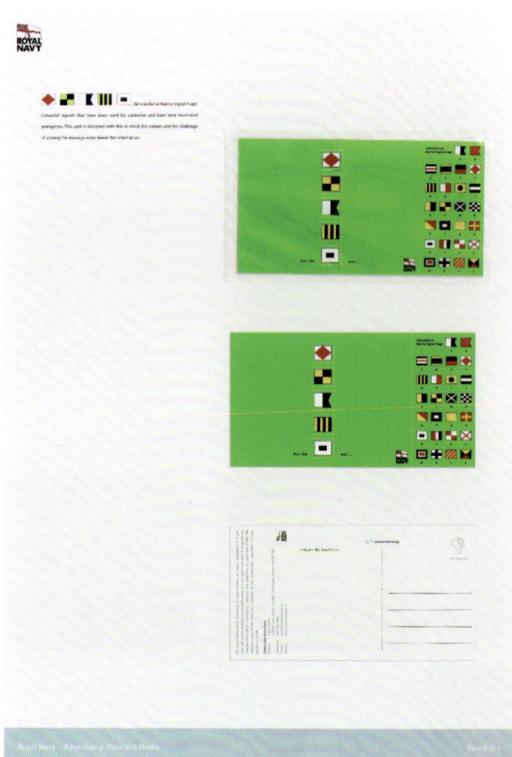

Commendation

Student
Kerry Bilton

Tutors
David Bullers
Simon Gomes
Keith Hume

College
Doncaster College

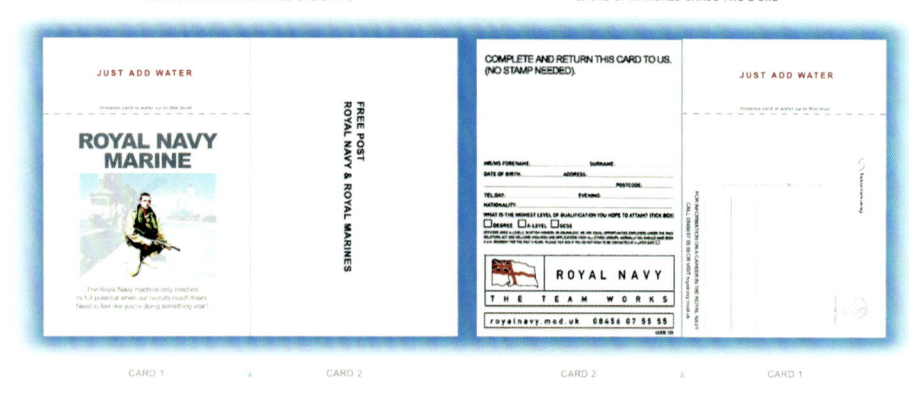

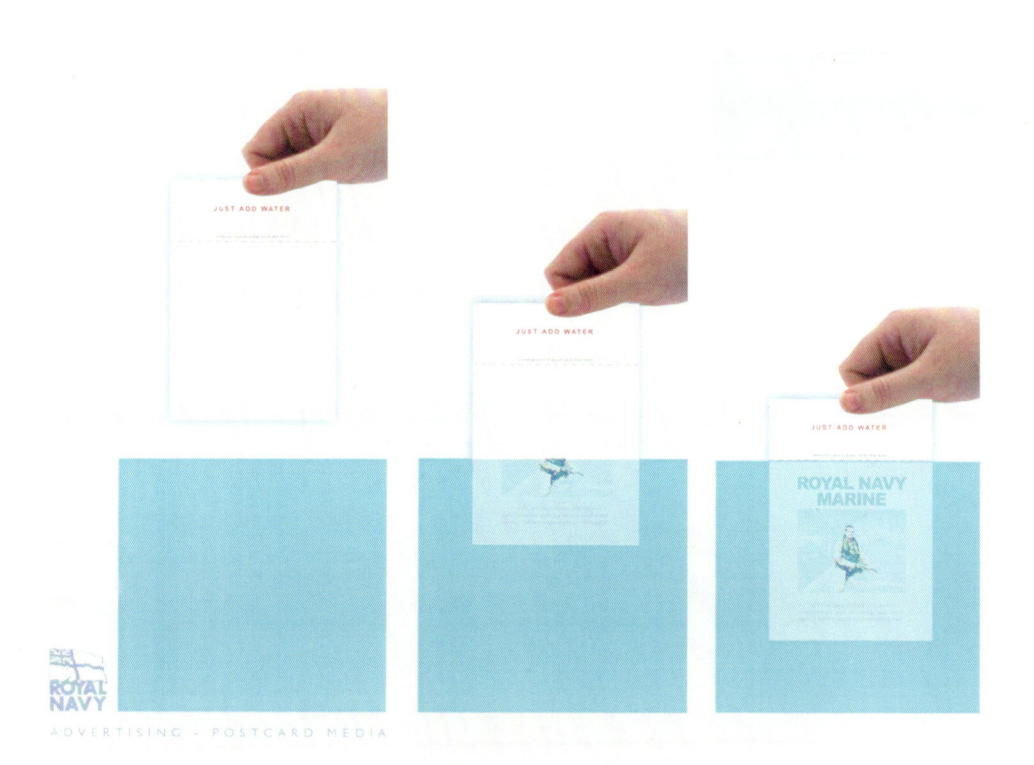

Student
Lisa Balm

Tutors
Guy Lawrence
Widge Hunt
Malcolm Swatridge

College
Somerset College
of Art and Technology

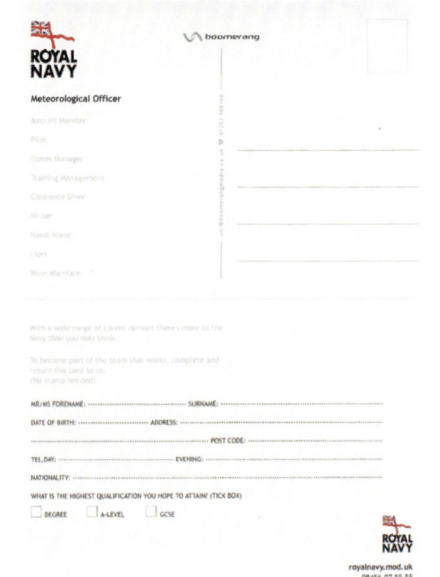

Students
Charlotte Bond
Chris Day
Emma Lewis

Tutors
Frank Holmes
Jon Dytor
Nick Holmes
Dave Sturdy

College
University of Gloucestershire

018

Students
Anna Ines Briano
Teresa Marcos Franco
Alberto Noda

Tutors
Marcelo Montes
Jose Maria de Armas

College
The School Agency

Students
Maria Crompton
Tamsin Garbutt

Tutor
Andy Bainbridge

College
University of Central Lancashire

Students
Belen De Azcarate
Rodrigo Lopez Caruana
Jorge Miguel Rodrigo Blanco

Tutors
Marcelo Montes
Chus Isidro

College
The School Agency

Students
Paul Bakker
Sebastiaan Kenter
Bies Vermeulen

Tutors
Dave Morris
Marien de Goffau

College
School for Commercial
Communication

Student
Claire Holden

Tutors
Jan Fitzpatrick
Brian Shaw

College
Edinburgh's Telford College

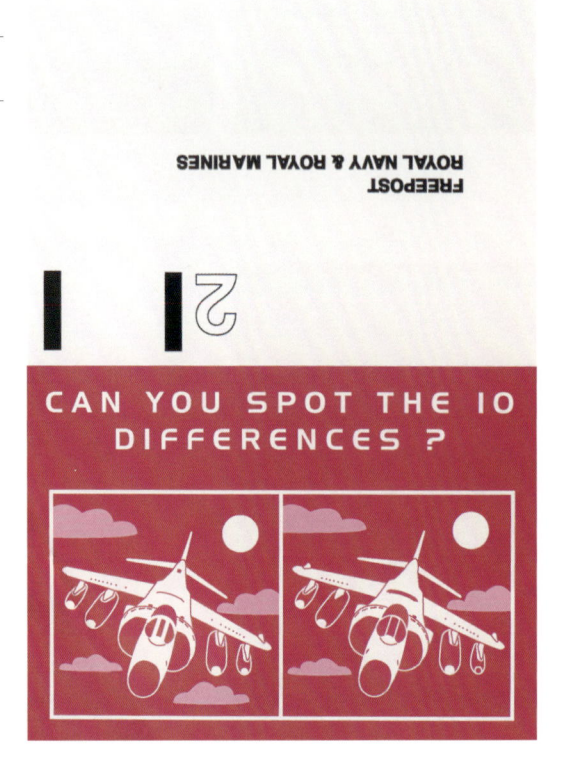

020

Students
Sarah Dutton
Louise Halliwell

Tutors
Andy Bainbridge
Ron Bray

College
University of Central Lancashire

Broaden your horizons

20% of new recruits go on to follow a Naval career in medicine.

Student
Robert Ward

Tutor
Andy Bainbridge

College
University of Central Lancashire

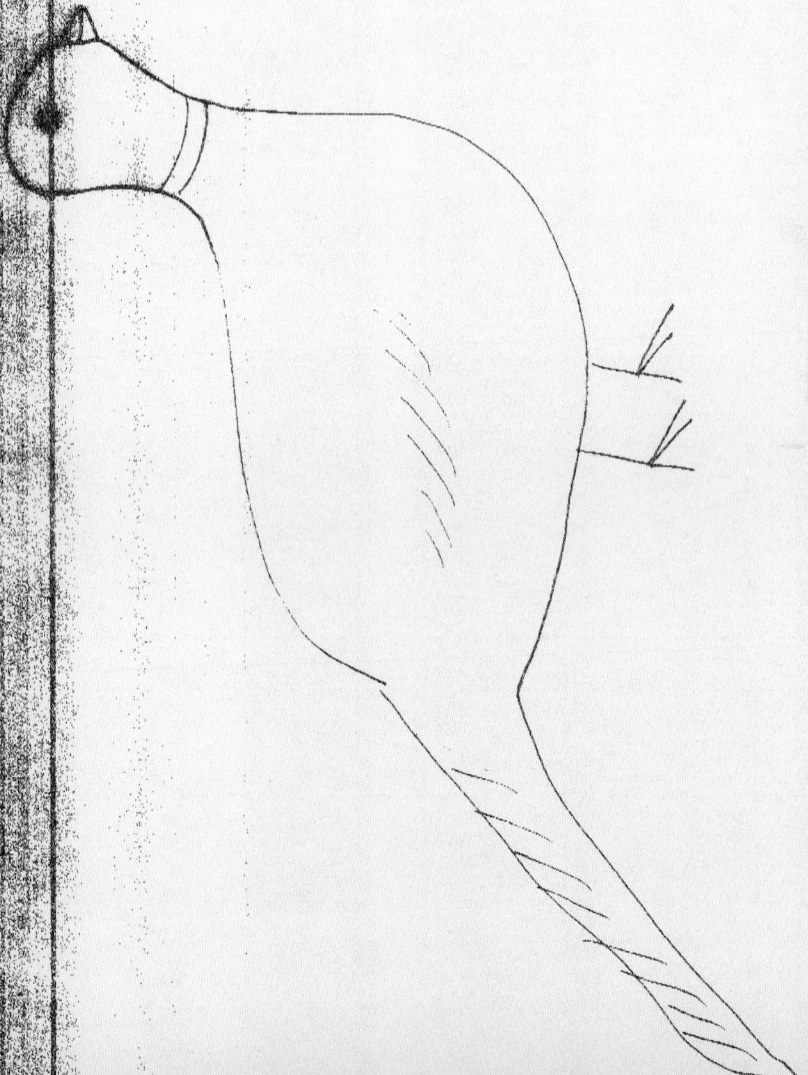

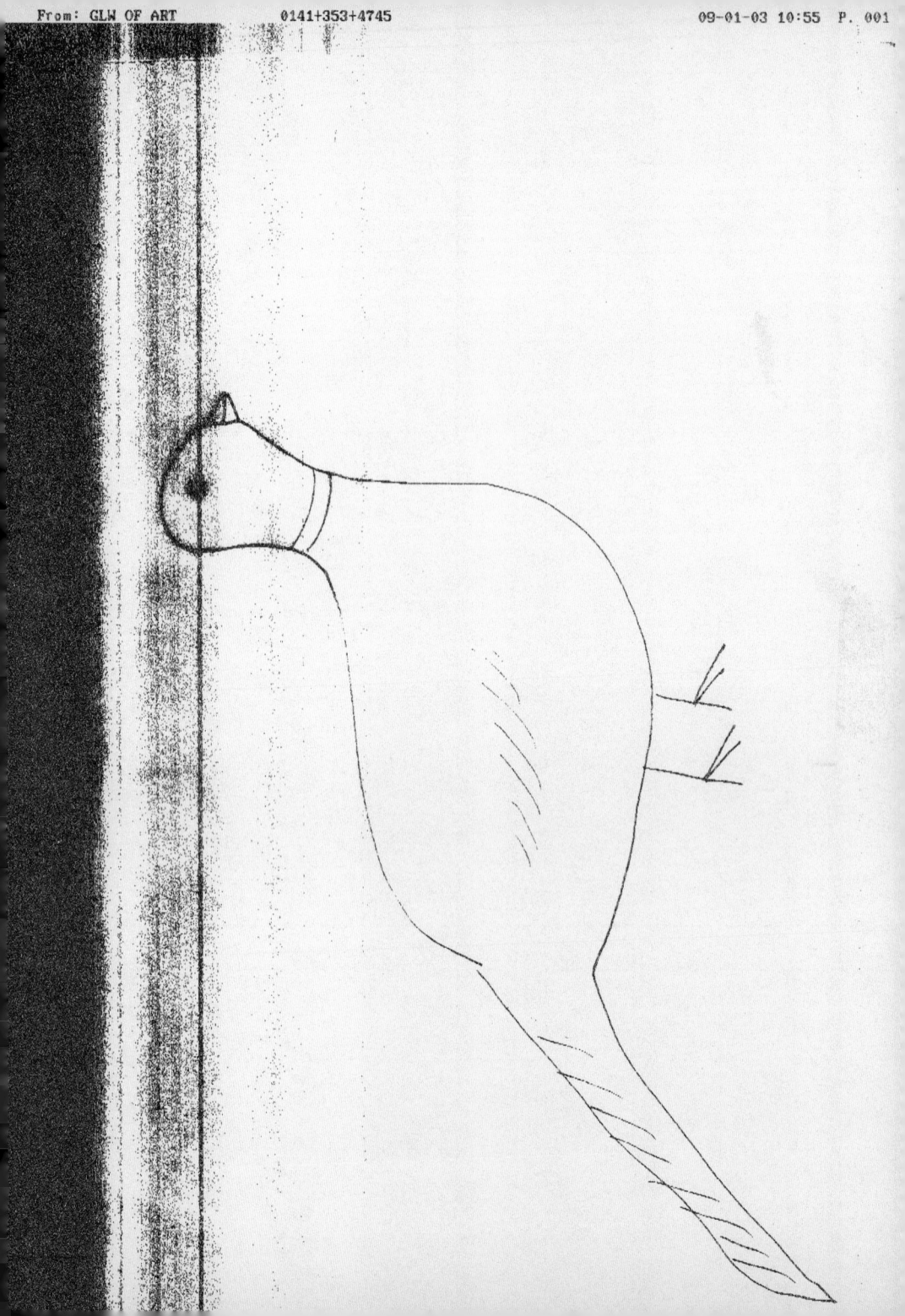

SPONSORED BY
THE NATIONAL MAGAZINE COMPANY
AND VIACOM OUTDOOR

ADVERTISING – TRANSPORT MEDIA

THE BRIEF TO DESIGN AN ADVERTISING CAMPAIGN FOR GOOD HOUSEKEEPING TO BE SHOWN ON BUSES AROUND THE UK, WITH AN AIM TO GET YOUNGER PEOPLE TO TAKE A FRESH LOOK AT THE MAGAZINE.

JUDGES' COMMENTS BUS ADVERTISING IS A CHALLENGE. A SUCCESSFUL DESIGN NEEDS TO BE CLEAR AND WELL BRANDED. MANY ENTRIES CONVEYED THE RIGHT MESSAGE BUT NOT WITH A DESIGN THAT WOULD WORK ON A BUS. THE WINNING ENTRY EMPLOYED A VERY CREATIVE USE OF THE 'DROP SECTION' OF THE T-SIDE TO GET THE MESSAGE ACROSS. **STEVE COX**

GETTING GIRLS TO BUY THEIR MUM'S CHOICE OF MAGAZINE ON A BUS SIDE IS NO EASY TASK… A LOT OF THE ENTRIES ANSWERED THE BRIEF TOO SAFELY. THE STRONG ONES MADE THE BUS SIDE SHAPE WORK TOGETHER WITH THE IDEA. **CLAUDIA SOUTHGATE**

I WAS HOPING THAT SOMEONE WOULD CONVINCE ME TO GO OUT AND BUY GOOD HOUSEKEEPING… THEY NEARLY DID… AS A STUDENT YOU HAVE TO PUSH YOUR WORK – I'D RATHER SEE FRESH, SIMPLE, OUTRAGEOUS IDEAS THAN SAFE ONES THAT WOULD RUN. SAFE ONES ARE WHAT YOU DO WHEN YOU GET A JOB. **VERITY FENNER**

THE WINNING ENTRY WAS THE MOST INVENTIVE IDEA, THE ONLY ONE THAT TRULY INDICATED THAT THERE MIGHT BE A SLIGHTLY MORE RISQUÉ UNDERSIDE TO WHAT IS SEEN AS A FAIRLY WHOLESOME MAGAZINE. **PAUL GRUBB**

Claudia Southgate
Bartle Bogle Hegarty

Steve Cox
Viacom Outdoor

Denny Barnes
National Magazines

Verity Fenner
Bartle Bogle Hegarty

Paul Grubb
Duckworth Finn
Grubb Waters

First

Students
Alex Braxton
Mark Ward

Tutors
Maggie Gallagher
Clive Challis
Zelda Malan

College
Central Saint Martins/
College of Art and Design

Second

Student
Claire Yates

Tutors
David Beaugeard
Paul Minott

College
Bath Spa University College

025

Commendation

Student
Hannah Tourle

Tutors
Guy Lawrence
Widge Hunt
Malcolm Swatridge

College
Somerset College
of Art and Technology

Students
Sarah Harris
Gary Williams

Tutors
Leah Klein
Julie Wright
John Merriman

College
Buckinghamshire Chilterns
University College

Students
Caterina Calabro
Andrea Mineo
Anna Palama

Tutor
Valentina Majocchi

College
Accademia di
Communicazione

WOULD IT HELP IF YOU WERE BEAUTIFUL?

Yes, but it'd be even more helpful if you could print our numbers (07811453803 - Rob 07977150316 - Nick) and get us a placement at Kesselskramer. please. THANKS.

SPONSORED BY
EHS BRANN

EHS BRANN

ADVERTISING CAMPAIGN – OPEN BRIEF

THE BRIEF PRODUCE AN ADVERTISING CAMPAIGN TO ANNOUNCE THE LAUNCH OF THE NEW PEUGEOT 206 GTI 180. CREATE A BIG SPLASH, POSITIONING IT AS THE NEW HOT-HATCH BENCHMARK. THE BUDGET WOULD NOT BE ENOUGH FOR A LARGE BROADCAST CAMPAIGN, SO OTHER MEDIUMS MUST BE CONSIDERED.

JUDGES' COMMENTS THIS CAR IS NOT MAX POWER: IT'S NOT ABOUT GIRLS, GO FASTER STRIPES AND SPEED. IT'S FAR MORE SOPHISTICATED THAN THAT. THE WINNING ENTRIES REFLECTED THIS VERY INTELLIGENTLY! WELL DONE. **OLIVER GRIFFIN**

WE WERE LOOKING FOR A BIG BANG FROM A SMALL BUCK. THE MOST IMPORTANT INGREDIENT WAS TO 'CUT THROUGH' WITH IMPACT WHILE BEING RELEVANT. THE WINNER COMMUNICATED THE SALES MESSAGE WITH REAL CHARM. IT WAS A SINGLE-MINDED EXECUTION THAT HAD PLENTY OF STAND OUT. **XANTHOS CHRISTODOULOU**

MANY OF THE ENTRIES SHOWED GREAT CREATIVE THINKING AND IN A FEW CASES IDEAS THAT CAPTURED THE IMAGINATION OF THE HARD NOSED PROFESSIONAL JUDGES BECAUSE OF THEIR ORIGINALITY OF THOUGHT. **PHIL JONES**

I'M A STRONG ADVOCATE OF SIMPLE THINKING, SO I WAS REALLY LOOKING FOR ADS THAT I UNDERSTOOD IMMEDIATELY… THE WINNER WAS STRONG VISUALLY GIVING IT A SALIENT IDENTITY. IT AVOIDED THE SPEED CLICHÉ BUT STILL CONVEYED THAT THE PEUGEOT WAS A PERFORMANCE CAR. **FRANCESCA NEWLAND**

Xanthos Christodoulou
EHS Brann

Phil Jones
EHS Brann

Oliver Griffin
Peugeot

Nick Wootton
J Walter Thompson

Francesca Newland
Campaign

First

Students
Kathrina Hahn
Stephen Howell

Tutors
David Morris
Zelda Malan
Lyndon Mallet

College
Buckinghamshire Chilterns
University College

Motorway road signs

Billboard

Second

Students
Tushar Date
Kevin Koller

Tutor
Renetta Welty

College
Miami Ad School

Commendation

Student
John Aitchison

Tutors
Leah Klein
Julie Wright
Lyndon Mallet

College
Buckinghamshire Chilterns
University College

front The card is stuck to the drivers side wing mirror on parked cars. Specific cars will be targeted e.g: VW Golf, Citroen Saxo, Ford Focus, BMW 3 series.

Students
Rick Dodds
Lisa Mitchell

Tutors
Zelda Malan
David Morris
Lyndon Mallet

College
Buckinghamshire Chilterns
University College

Student
Emma Davey

Tutors
John Lowe
David Osbaldestin

College
Birmingham Institute
of Art and Design

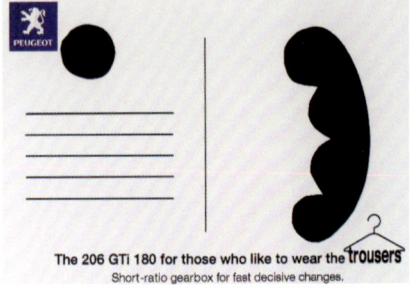

032

Student
David Ryan
Ben Scott

Tutors
Richard Haydon
Mike Comley

College
West Thames College

Steven Crouch   Kent Institute of Art and Design – Illustration.

Can I draw a ferret?

does it look like it?

SPONSORED BY
PRET A MANGER

★ PRET A MANGER ★

AMBIENT MEDIA

THE BRIEF BUILD THE PRET BRAND TO NEW CUSTOMERS THROUGH AN AMBIENT CAMPAIGN BY KEEPING THE BRAND FRESH AND RELEVANT. AS PRET'S PERSONALITY IS NON-CORPORATE AND SLIGHTLY QUIRKY, THIS SHOULD BE REFLECTED IN THE SOLUTION BY MAKING PEOPLE THINK AS WELL AS MAKING THEM SMILE.

JUDGES' COMMENTS THE BENCH SOLUTION HAD A REAL CHARM, USED A GREAT TONE OF VOICE AND WAS EXTREMELY RELEVANT TO THE BRAND. IT HAD BEEN CAREFULLY WORKED THROUGH A NUMBER OF DIFFERENT APPLICATIONS. I WAS REALLY IMPRESSED WITH THE OVERALL STANDARD OF CREATIVITY… MANY OF THE CONCEPTS PRESENTED WOULD GIVE CREATIVE AGENCIES A RUN FOR THEIR MONEY!
CHRISTINA WRIGHT

I KNOW SANDWICH BOARD MEN ARE AS OLD AS THE HILLS BUT IT MANAGED TO GET THE TONE JUST RIGHT; HUMOROUS AND ATTENTION GRABBING WHILST AT THE SAME TIME HIGHLIGHTING THE 'HEALTHY' ASPECT OF PRET'S PRODUCT RANGE. ON THE WHOLE, MY ONLY CRITICISM WOULD BE THAT MORE CREATIVE RISKS COULD HAVE BEEN TAKEN WITH SOME OF THE WORK. WITH THE MEDIA LANDSCAPE AS CLUTTERED AS IT IS, ACTIVITY REALLY NEEDS TO STAND OUT FROM THE BACKGROUND 'NOISE'. **FLOYD HAYES**

Floyd Hayes
Cunning Stunts

Julian Metcalfe
Pret a Manger

Christina Wright
Pret a Manger

Jim Thornton
Mother

First

Student
Esther Alcaide

Tutors
Kate Bashford
Guy Preston

College
Barnet College

036

Second

Student
Joe Harries

Tutors
Cath Caldwell
Amanda Lester

College
Central Saint Martins/
College of Art and Design

Street Cleaning / Reverse Graffiti

To promote Pret around the city I wanted to do something that emphasised the natural and fresh qualities of Pret's products. Busy urban streets are often quite dirty places, and when the council clean the pavements properly, it always makes a huge difference.

My idea is to use this street-cleaning process as advertising, using stencils of a simple sandwich shape to clean selected parts of pavements around the city as a kind of 'reverse graffiti'.

The designs would erode naturally over time and could be replaced regularly, mirroring the fresh sandwiches produced each morning.

The shapes would also vary in size to fit in with the specific area of pavement.

This would communicate Pret's position as a fresh change from other sandwich shops, a natural element standing out from the rest, whilst also appearing sensitive to the existing environment (cleaning the streets rather than covering them with ads).

Commendation

Students
Nick Dell'anno
Will Thacker

Tutors
Andrew Baker
Bren Nevin
Bev Whitehead

College
Surrey Institute of Art and Design University College at Epsom

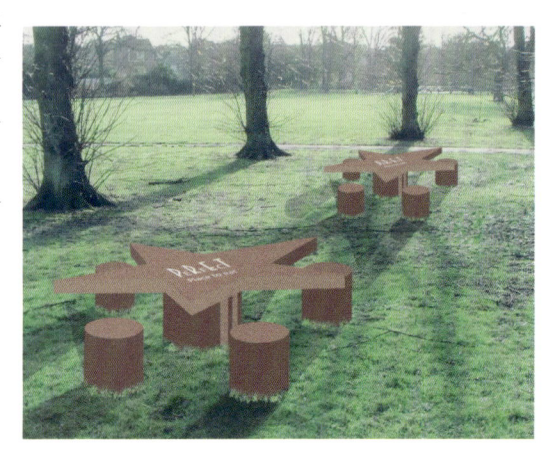

Students
Rhavin Lutchman
Tim Wood

Tutors
Alice Kavounas Taylor
Digby Atkinson

College
Falmouth College of Arts

People dressed up in pigeon costumes will distribute packets of birdseed in the city centre.

Student
Philippa Morrice

Tutor
Amanda Lester

College
Central Saint Martins/
College of Art and Design

Student
Rodrigo Fernandes

Tutor
Tom Lunt

College
Miami Ad School

039

Student
Wai Yuen Leung

Tutors
Sannia Ho
Simon Wang

College
Hong Kong Institute
of Vocational Education

Students
Scott Hayes
Maari Thrall

Tutors
Norm Grey
Mike Weed

College
The Creative Circus

Air Fresheners smelling of fresh food will be hung in taxies and buses, reading "Breath In" and "Pret a Manger...Passion for the Natural".

Students
Paul Kinsella
Cynthia Wong

Tutors
Lin Sinclair
Mike Moran
Mark Lamey

College
University of Central Lancashire

RANALD GRAHAM
VIS. COMM.
GLASGOW
SCHOOL
OF ART

BURN, BURN, BURN

SPONSORED BY GLENFIDDICH

BRAND IDENTITY AND DEVELOPMENT

THE BRIEF DEVELOP A NEW AND DESIRABLE WHISKY CONCEPT FOR A YOUNGER AUDIENCE THAT WILL INTRODUCE THEM TO THE GLENFIDDICH EXPERIENCE. REMIX THE GLENFIDDICH BRAND TO CREATE A SUB-BRAND WHICH KEEPS THE EXCLUSIVITY OF THE ORIGINAL, WHILE CATERING FOR TODAY'S URBAN, STYLISH DRINKERS.

JUDGES' COMMENTS IT WAS DIFFICULT TO RECONCILE THE REQUIREMENTS OF THE BRIEF WITH THOSE EXPECTED OF A TRADITIONAL BRAND IDENTITY EXERCISE. WITH WIT, DESIGN QUALITY AND EXECUTION, THE WINNER WAS A WELL THOUGHT THROUGH PROJECT WITH EVERY ELEMENT ACHIEVING A HIGH STANDARD. **MICHAEL DENNY**

I WAS LOOKING FOR ENTRIES THAT PUSHED THE BOUNDARIES OF HOW TO PRESENT WHISKY WITHOUT LOSING THE PREMIUM VALUES… THE MAJORITY USED THE MIX OF GRAPHICS AND PRODUCT DESIGN VERY WELL. THE BEST IDEAS REQUIRED NO EXPLANATION. **ELWYN GLADSTONE**

THE OVERALL ABILITY TO TREAT THE PROJECT AS TOTAL BRANDING RATHER THAN JUST A LOGO OR A PACK WAS IMPRESSIVE. STRONG BRANDING, IMAGINATION AND AN ANARCHIC LINK WITH THE PARENT BRAND MADE THE FIRST PRIZE-WINNER STAND OUT. **GEOFF HALPIN**

Geoff Halpin
Identica

Katrina Wateridge
Glenfiddich

Alison Tomlin
Carter Wong Tomlin

Michael Denny
Roundel

Elwyn Gladstone
Glenfiddich

First

Student
Ben Cox

Tutors
Guy Lawrence
Widge Hunt
Malcolm Swatridge

College
Somerset College
of Art and Technology

044

Second

Student
Kim Clark

Tutors
Malcolm Jobling
Nick Jeeves

College
Dunstable College

Student
Gareth Chubb

Tutors
Judith Hills
Gerald Emanuel

College
University of Glamorgan

Student
Mattias Lindstedt

Tutor
William Easton

College
Berghs School
of Communication

Student
Matthew Davies

Tutors
Steve Burdett
Debbie Douglas

College
University of Northumbria
at Newcastle

Student
Paul Roberts

Tutor
Alan Thomas

College
University of Lincoln

047

Student
Brad Logan

Tutors
Steve Burdett
Debbie Douglas

College
University of Northumbria at Newcastle

Student
Tom Stimpson

Tutors
Phillipa Wood
Chris Dune

College
University of Lincoln

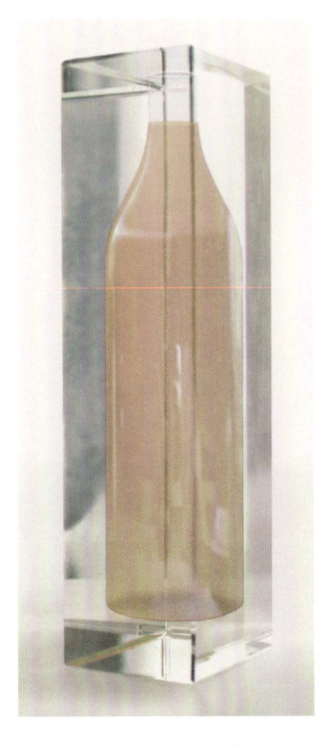

048

Student
Alex Griffin

Tutor
Roger Gould

College
The Arts Institute
Bournemouth

04/02/2003 15:02 441312216100 ECA VIS COMM PAGE 03

Sarah, 21,
from Edinburgh.
Likes pencils, helvetica
and thinking up ideas

WOULD IT HELP IF YOU WERE BEAUTIFUL
SARAH LONGWORTH - EDINBURGH COLLEGE OF ART

SPONSORED BY CORUS

CORUS STEEL PACKAGING

THE BRIEF – BOTANICS TO CREATE A NEW PACKAGING DESIGN FOR MEN'S PRODUCTS WITHIN THIS RANGE, COMBINING THE BRAND'S CURRENT IDENTITY WITH BOTH MASCULINE APPEAL AND GREATER SHELF PRESENCE.

JUDGE'S COMMENT THE SIMPLICITY OF THE WINNER'S EXECUTION EXPRESSED BEAUTIFULLY THAT BOTANICS IS ABOUT THE 'PURE POWER OF PLANTS'. IT CLEARLY COMMUNICATED THE BRAND'S MINIMAL BUT POWERFUL AESTHETIC. **BARBARA CALDERWOOD**

THE BRIEF – HUGO BOSS FRAGRANCE CREATE NEW PRODUCT USAGE OF THE HUGO BRAND WITH AN INNOVATIVE AND AESTHETICALLY UNCONVENTIONAL OBJECT.

JUDGE'S COMMENT USING A PLUG-IN REFILL SYSTEM WHICH BECAME A PORTABLE DISPENSER IN ITS OWN RIGHT MADE THE WINNING DESIGN A VERY STRONG IDEA. **KEREN HOUSE**

THE BRIEF – VIRGIN ATLANTIC AIRWAYS CREATE A MORE INTERESTING, ENJOYABLE AND UNIQUELY VIRGIN ATLANTIC MEAL TRAY WHICH IS BOTH ENVIRONMENTALLY SOUND AND USER FRIENDLY FOR BOTH CREW AND CUSTOMER.

JUDGE'S COMMENT A REAL INNOVATION. THE DESIGN GIVES THE CUSTOMER THE CHOICE OF VIEWING ONLY THE FOOD THEY WANT TO EAT. IT ALSO CONCEALS THE REMAINS OF THE PREVIOUS COURSE WHEN YOU PROGRESS THROUGH THE MEAL. THIS GIVES BOTH RITUAL AND FREEDOM OF CHOICE. **JOE FERRY**

Allen McDowell
Crown Cork & Seal

Ben Hargreaves
New Design

Ian Ritchie
Jones Knowles Ritchie

Martin Bunce
Tin Horse

Wil Shoenmakers
Procter & Gamble

Joe Ferry
Virgin Atlantic Airways

Barbara Calderwood
Boots PLC

Bill Walsgrove
Big Idea

Keren House
Siebert Head

Henk Lip
Corus Packaging Plus

Botanics
First

Student
Pasquale Volpe

Tutor
Valentina Majocchi

College
Accademia di Communicazione

BOTANICS
The pure power of plants

In the new design if the product regarding
the range man botanic, is Nature becoming container.

It is a twig remade in a modern key
More modern,
Hi-tech by still, all by still.

Simple, clean natural, it behaves as a vegetal.

If carved, cut, marked, it let spill its life sap.
So, if some sap comes out from the package, it means
that, closed in the still twig, there's sap: the same sap
which, coming out from the cap or the supply, you use as
cosmetic and broadcast "the Pure Power of Plants".

The range is made by a family of still cylinders with a
same light inclination and characterized by an evident
cut, with arrogance, breaks the elegant continuity of the
cylindric shape.

Inside the the cut, the walls are coarse, texturized and
from these walls some "sap" comes out, a kind of sap
made by a drop of green resin.

The contrapposition between the tecnological process
given by still and the green resin sap, emphasize the high
quality and security of the product deeply studied, which
preserves and guarantees the totally natural principles and
benefits of the best plants used.

The dimensions of the cylindric containers and the different
supplies or caps changes as the product changes.

The elegant screen printing on the packaging is a range
of continuity with the previous ones in order to guarantee
the recognizability of the brand and its values.

Finally, its design allows an elegant play of
composition which remembers a minimum hi-tech garden.

Second

Student
Giulia Inaudi

Tutor
Valentina Majocchi

College
Accademia di Communicazione

Commendation

Student
Patricia Saavedra

Tutors
Bill Stewart
Claire Lockwood
Glyn Hawley

College
Sheffield Hallam University

The range of BOTANICS products for men, is presented in a packaging design based on a leaf shape, to give a strong visual message of **"the power of plants"**.

The nerves of the leaf suggest also a tree, and the six-pack muscles of a healthy and strong man, this detail combined with the natural color of steel, gives a masculine appearance to the product.

Student
Emily Hancock

Tutors
Bill Stewart
Glyn Hawley
Claire Lockwood

College
Sheffield Hallam University

BOTANICS
MEN'S BODY
the PURE POWER OF PLANTS

These are just a small selection of the Men's BOTANICS range which have been re-designed to give more shelf presence and to attract a wider male audience. The basis of the design is supported by images of strong rainforest trees and collosal buttresses which support the tree's powerful trunks.

Students
Hao He
Joo Young Park

Tutors
Bill Stewart
Claire Lockwood
Glyn Hawley

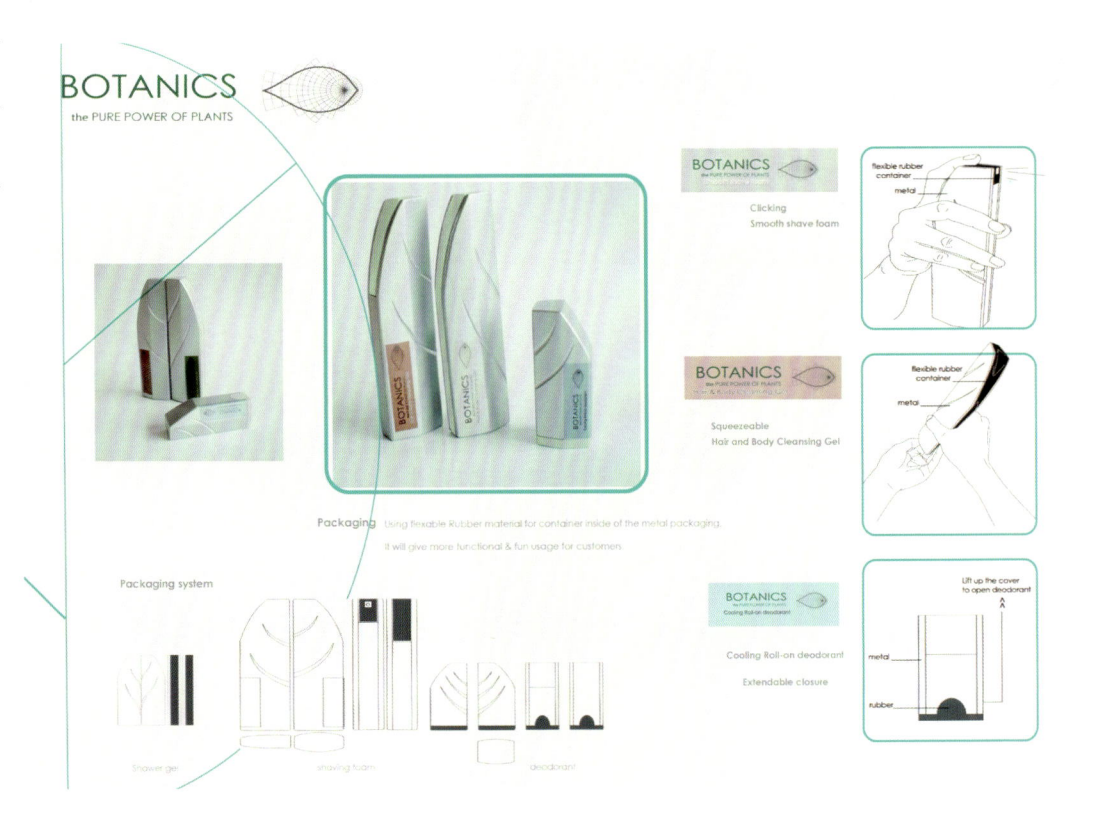

College
Sheffield Hallam University

BOTANICS
the PURE POWER OF PLANTS

BOTANICS
Clicking
Smooth shave foam

BOTANICS
Squeezeable
Hair and Body Cleansing Gel

BOTANICS
Cooling Roll-on deodorant
Extendable closure

Packaging: Using flexible Rubber material for container inside of the metal packaging. It will give more functional & fun usage for customers.

Packaging system

Shower gel · shaving foam · deodorant

Hugo by Hugo Boss
Fragrance
First

Students
Charlotte Hayes
Sam Lachlan

Tutors
David Beaugeard
Paul Minott

College
Bath Spa University College

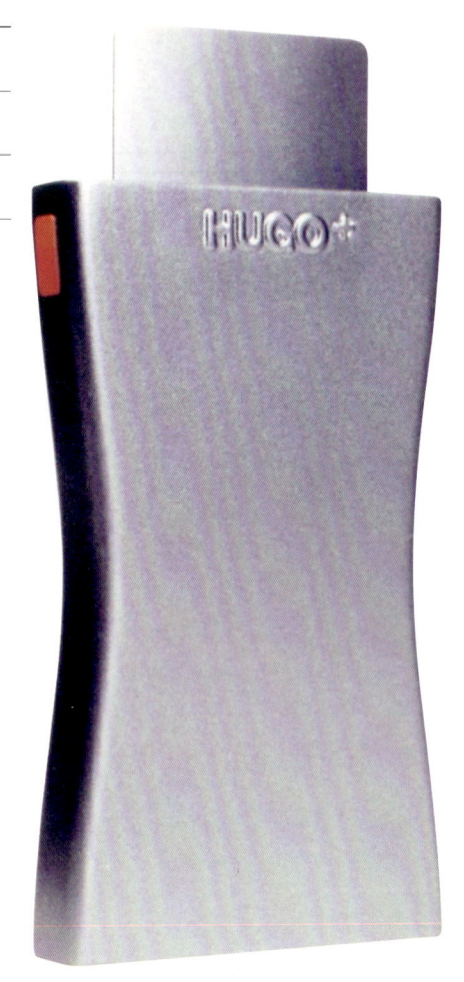

Holding up to 3ml of fragrance, the Charge Card is designed to be used again and again. When inserted into the Recharger the Charge Card is refilled in one motion.

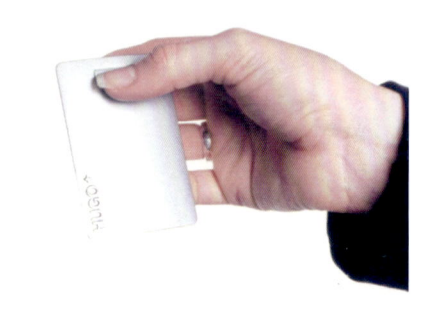

Second

Student
Tracey Brassington

Tutors
David Beaugeard
Paul Minott

College
Bath Spa University College

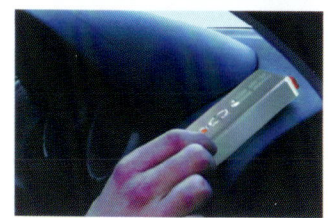

057

Commendation

Student
Keeley Foord

Tutors
Andrew Aloof
David Fowler

College
Hastings College of Arts and Technology

Student
Ooi Shur Ling

Tutor
Patricia Campbell

College
Lasalle-Sia College of the Arts

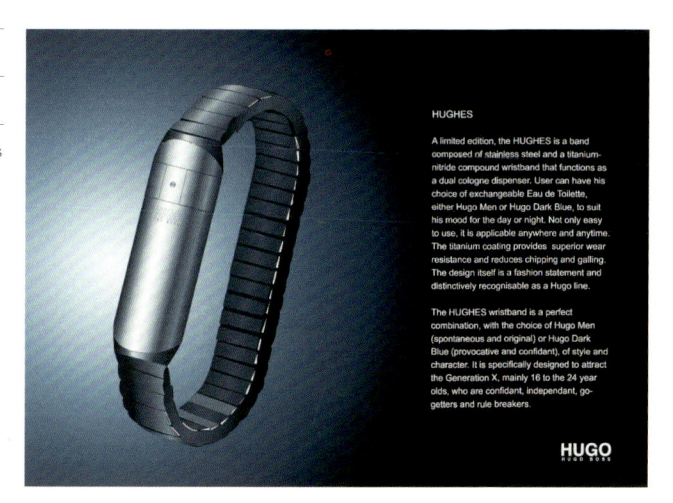

Student
Natalie Turner

Tutors
Bill Stewart
Claire Lockwood
Glyn Hawley

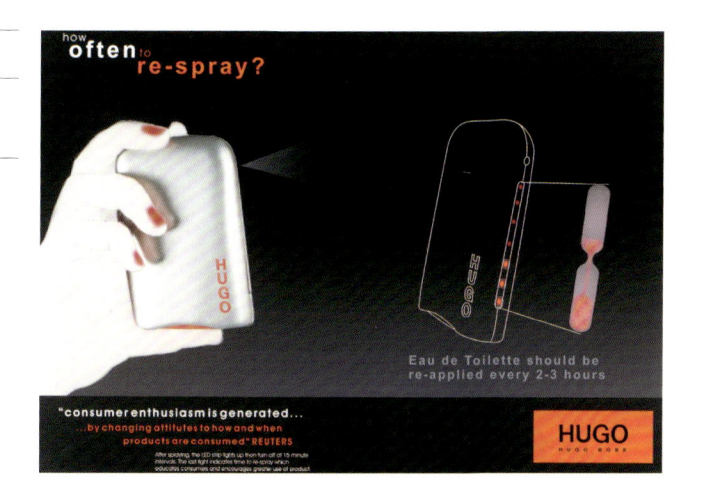

College
Sheffield Hallam University

059

**Virgin Atlantic Airways
First**

Student
Guenaelle Stulz

Tutor
Remy Jacquet

College
Ecole Cantonale
D'Art de Lausanne

starter

hot main course

fly around the plate ...

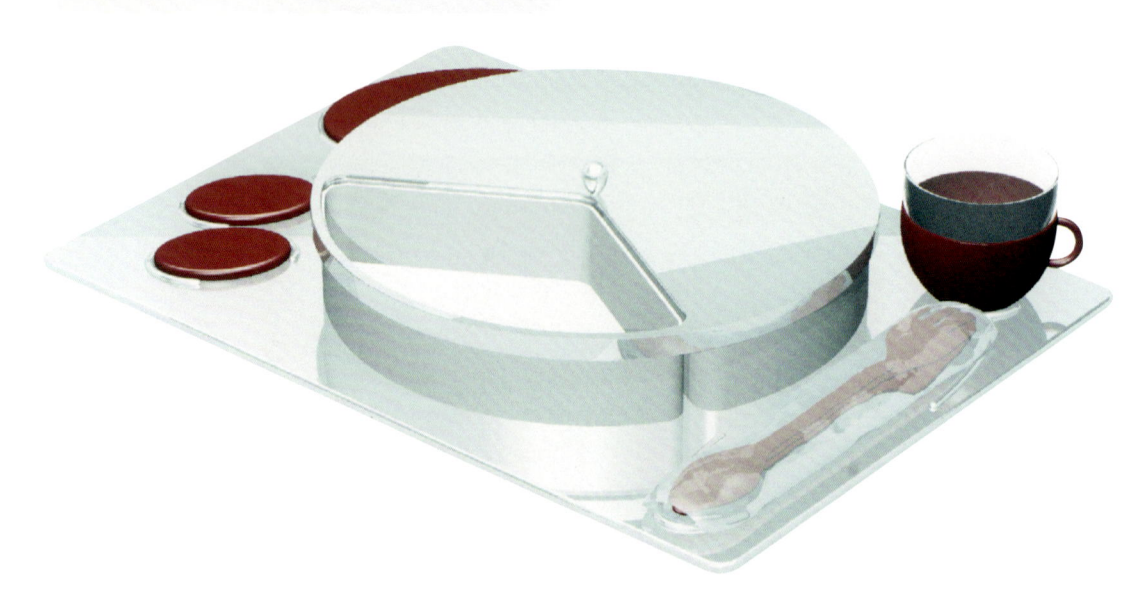

virgin atlantic

dessert

060

Second

Student
Pauline Bucher

Tutor
Remy Jacquet

College
Ecole Cantonale
D'Art de Lausanne

colors box

pleasure of the eyes
pleasure of eating

virgin atlantic

Second

Student
Nicole Gotti

Tutor
Remy Jacquet

College
Ecole Cantonale
D'Art de Lausanne

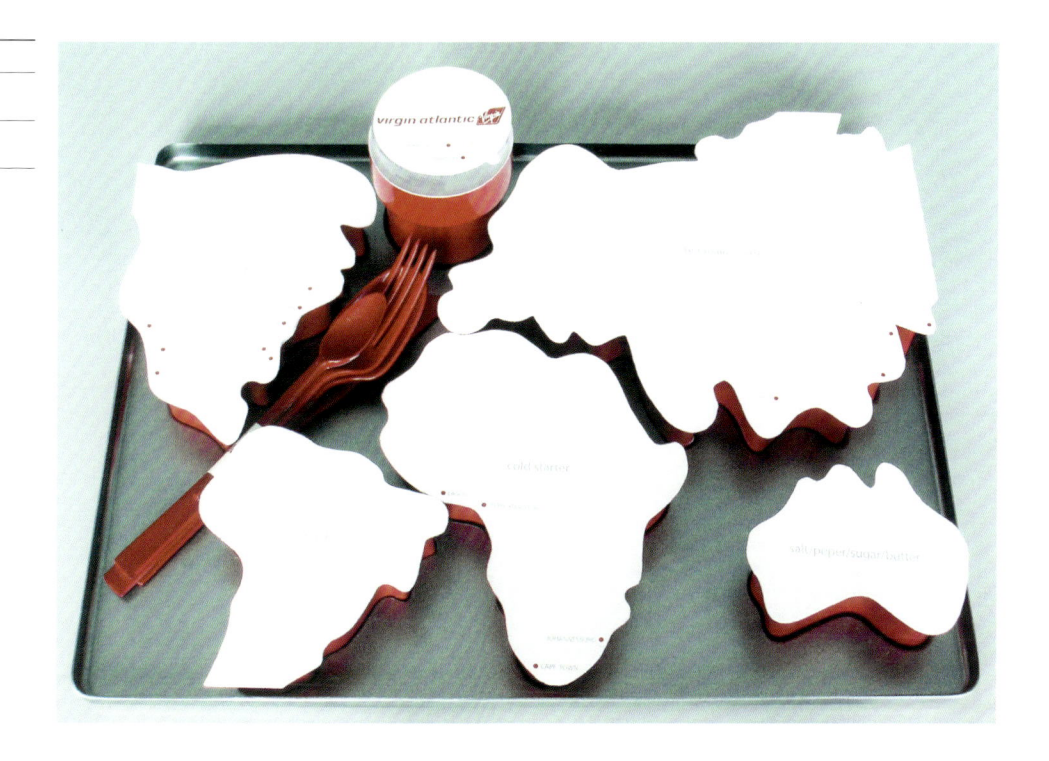

061

Commendation

Student
Daniel Smith

Tutors
Bill Stewart
Claire Lockwood
Glyn Hawley

College
Sheffield Hallam University

Student
Alan Pride

Tutors
Duncan Hepburn
Bjorn Rodnes

College
Napier University

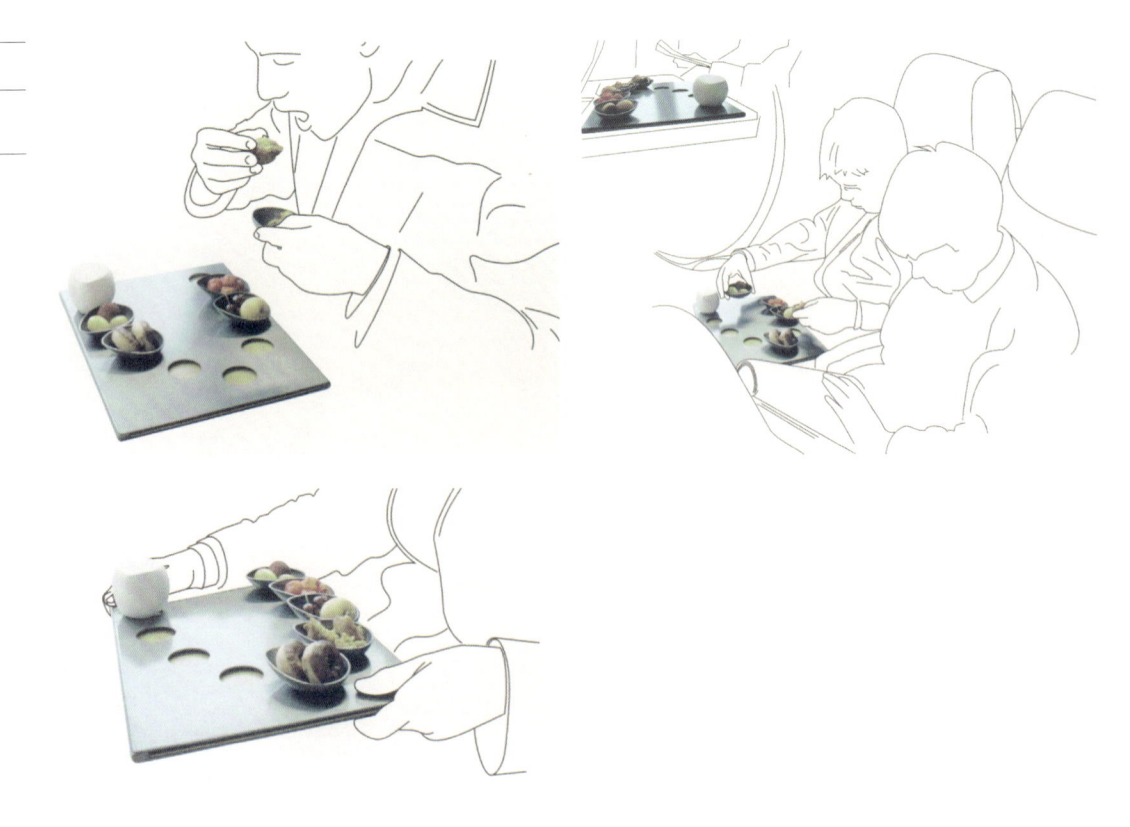

062

Students
Alan Dowds
John Russel
Laura Thomson

Tutors
Joanna Caskey
Liliana Rodriguez
Keith Moir

College
Glasgow College of Building and Printing

No but I can draw a dead fox.

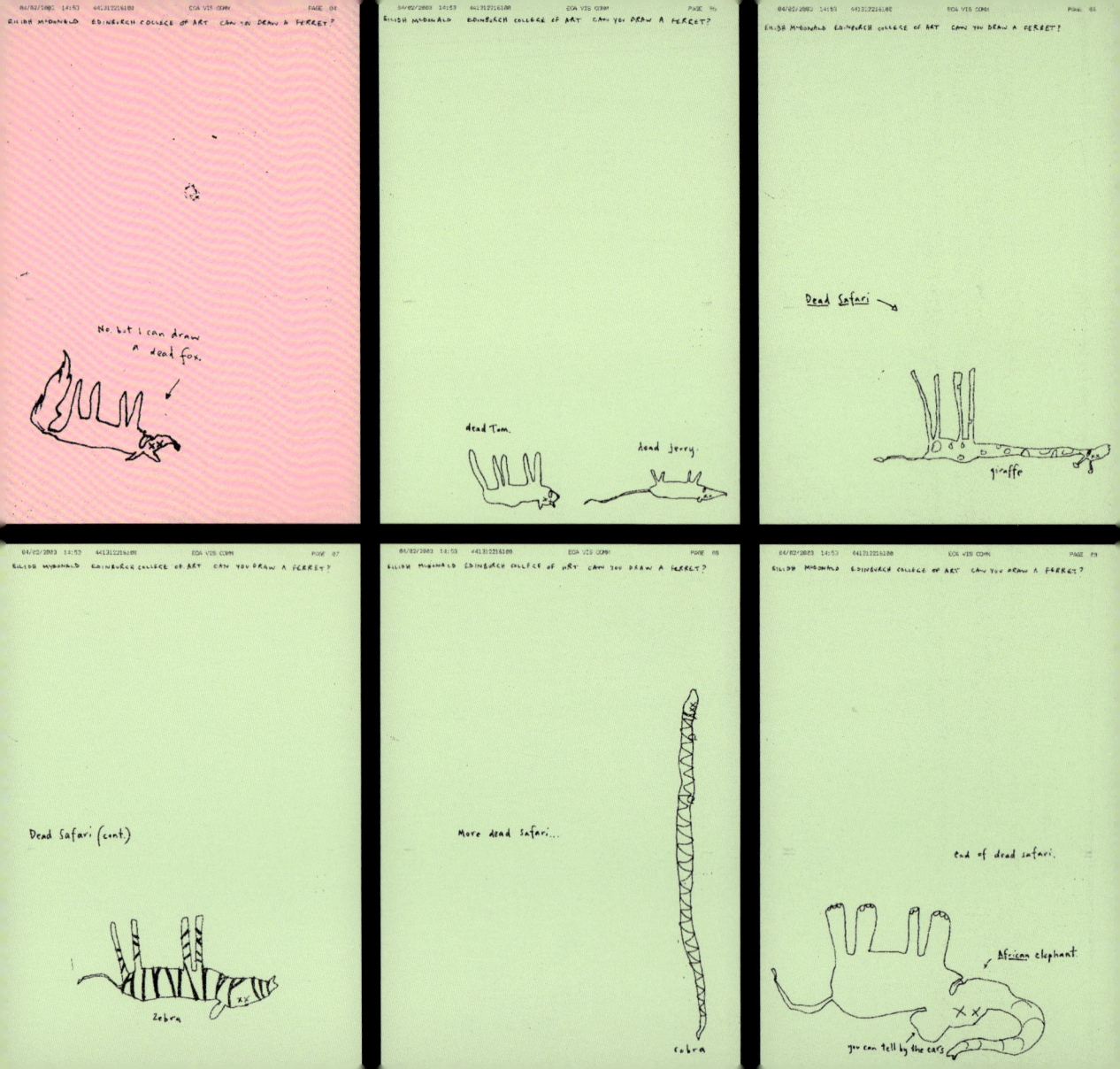

dead Tom.

dead Jerry.

Dead Safari

giraffe

Dead Safari (cont.)

zebra
xx

More dead safari...

cobra

end of dead safari.

African elephant.
xx
you can tell by the ears

SPONSORED BY ROYAL MAIL

DIRECT MAIL

THE BRIEF DEVELOP A DIRECT MAIL PACK AIMED AT STUDENTS LIVING AWAY FROM HOME TO PROVIDE INFORMATION AND ADVICE ON AVOIDING SEXUALLY TRANSMITTED INFECTIONS. EDUCATE THEM ABOUT THE RISKS WITHOUT BEING JUDGEMENTAL OR MORALISING ABOUT SEX IN ANY WAY.

JUDGES' COMMENTS THE WINNER SEEMED TO HIT THE STUDENT MENTALITY ON THE HEAD. THE STICKERS WOULD BE IRRESISTIBLE TO USE AND MAKE AN IMPORTANT POINT IN A FUN WAY, SPREADING THE MESSAGE AMONGST THEIR FRIENDS. A SMART, 'GET NOTICED' IDEA. **MIKE BOLES**

AN IMPRESSIVE ARRAY OF WORK… SUCCESSFUL ENTRANTS WERE THOSE THAT DELIVERED THE MESSAGE QUICKLY, WITH IMPACT TO ENGAGE PEOPLE, AND ALL THE WINNERS HAD SOMETHING THAT MEANT THEY WOULD GO BEYOND THE INITIAL STAGE. THE CUP WAS FUN – AS THE KITCHEN IS THE MAIN MEETING POINT IN HALLS OF RESIDENCE AND STUDENTS' HOUSES IT WOULD BE EXPOSED TO A WIDER AUDIENCE – WE WOULD LIKE TO HAVE SEEN A MALE VERSION AS WELL. **CHRIS ARNOLD**

THE ENTRANTS WERE REALLY ABLE TO GET BENEATH THE SKIN OF THE TARGET AUDIENCE. CREATIVE THEMES WERE BANG UP TO DATE MAKING IT DIFFICULT TO DIFFERENTIATE. SUCH A STRONG COMMITMENT TO THE MEDIUM IS VERY ENCOURAGING FOR THE FUTURE. **FRASER CHISHOLM**

Fraser Chisholm
Royal Mail

Mike Boles
Rainey Kelly Campbell Roalfe/Y&R

Chris Arnold
Feel

Juliet Hillier
FPA

First

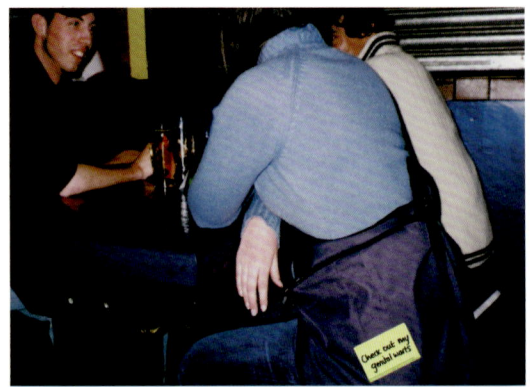

Students
Rebecca Hembrow
Rebecca Raftery

Tutors
Zelda Malan
David Morris
Lyndon Mallet

College
Buckinghamshire Chilterns
University College

Second

Students
Jo Forel
Petter Lublin

Tutors
Zelda Malan
Clive Challis
Maggie Gallagher

College
Central Saint Martins/
College of Art and Design

VNR 14 43 67

Instant STI home test.

fpa

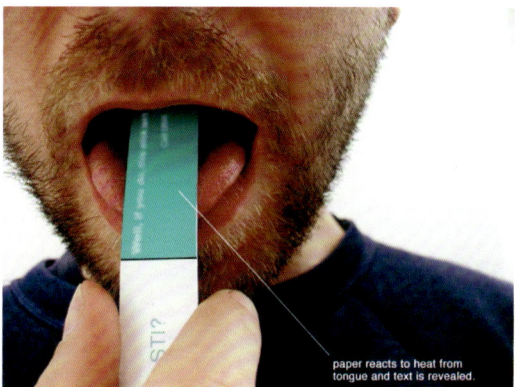

paper reacts to heat from tongue and text is revealed.

Second

Students
Rob Ferrara
Liz Franklin

Tutors
Leah Klein
Julie Wright
John Merriman

College
Buckinghamshire Chilterns
University College

Commendation

Students
Mahab Kazmi
Nikolai Kolstad

Tutors
Zelda Malan
Clive Challis
Maggie Gallagher

College
Central Saint Martins/
College of Art and Design

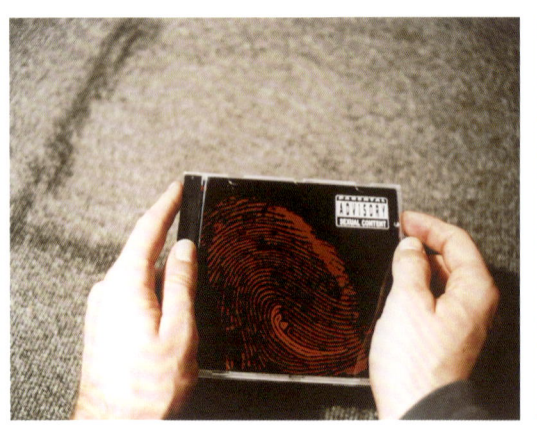

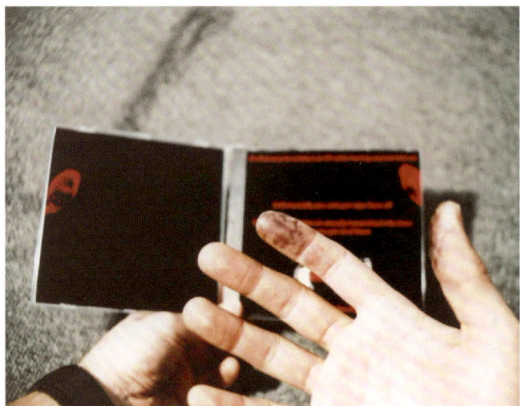

068

Students
Paul Brink
Gina Rossi

Tutor
Karen Birnholz

College
Miami Ad School

Student
Jesper Bange

Tutor
Kasia Rust

College
Central Saint Martins/
College of Art and Design

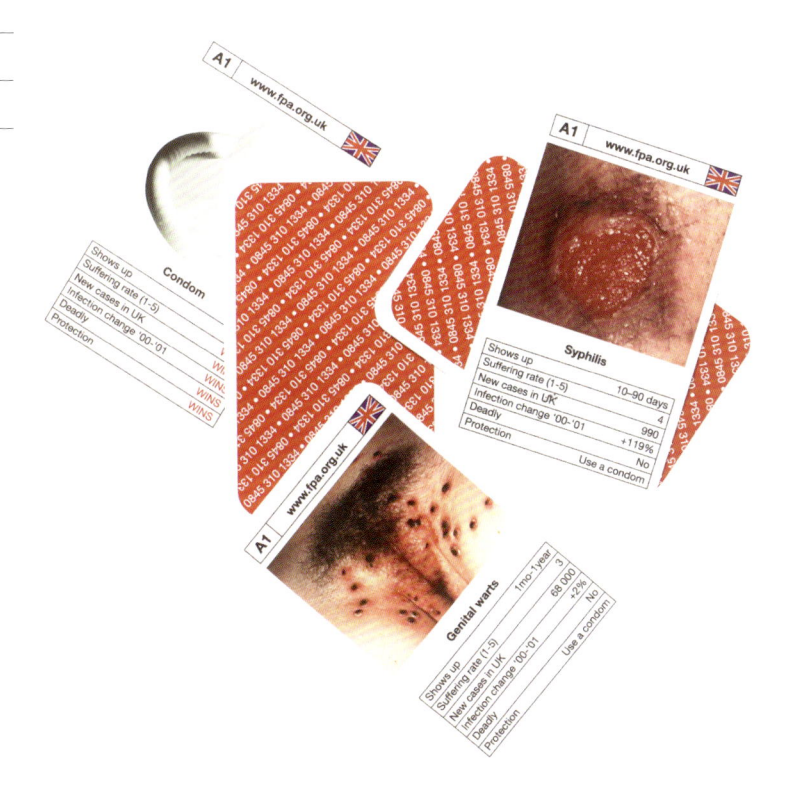

069

Students
Stella Deacon
Wei Yee Kung

Tutors
David Morris
Zelda Malan
Lyndon Mallet

College
Buckinghamshire Chilterns
University College

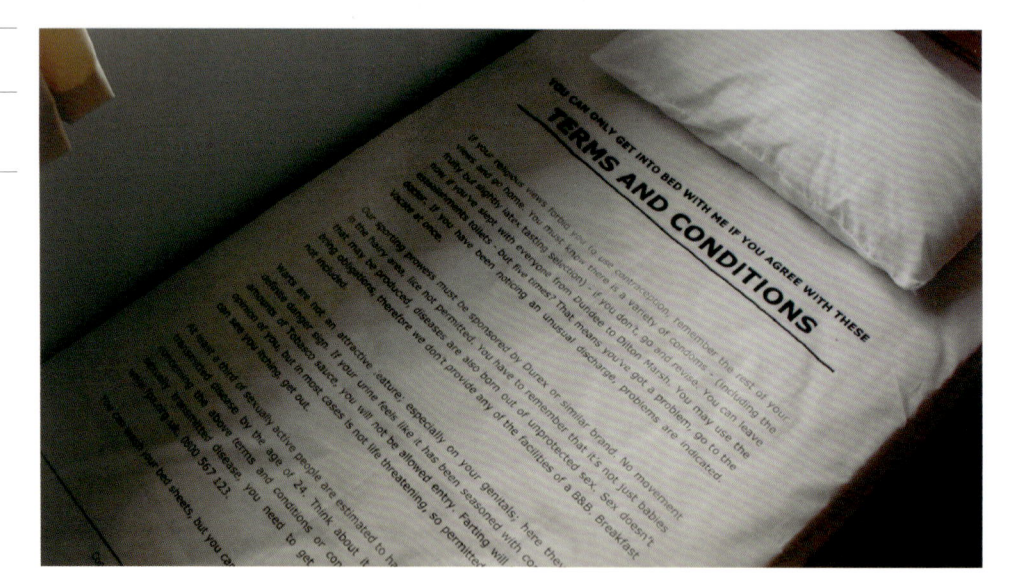

Student
Adam Parker

Tutor
Geoff Haddon

College
Middlesex University

Student
Karry Leung

Tutor
Amanda Lester

College
Central Saint Martins/
College of Art and Design

The approach is to deliver the message through the audience's interaction.

Students
Helen Lumby
Charlotte Smalley

Tutors
David Morris
Zelda Malan
Lyndon Mallet

College
Buckinghamshire Chilterns
University College

071

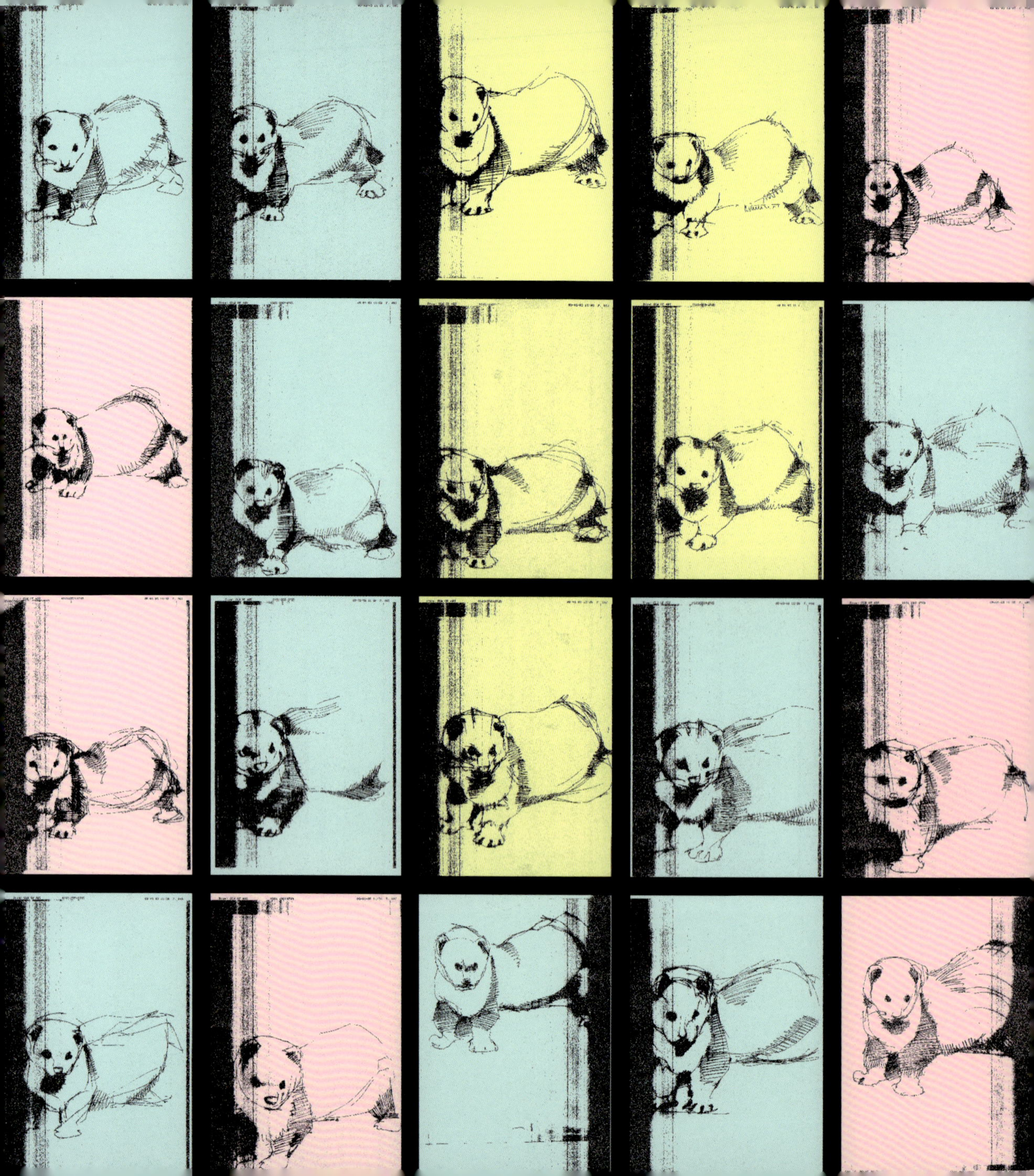

SPONSORED BY
TBWA\GGT

TBWA\GGT

DIRECT RESPONSE

THE BRIEF CREATE A DIRECT RESPONSE CAMPAIGN TO DRIVE STUDENTS TO OPEN A NATWEST STUDENT BANK ACCOUNT. THE CAMPAIGN MUST BE SIMPLE AND STRAIGHTFORWARD AND INCLUDE THREE MEDIA TYPES. CONSIDER THE PRACTICAL BENEFITS OF A NATWEST ACCOUNT BUT ALSO REFLECT THE INDEPENDENCE THAT COMES WITH STUDENT LIFE.

JUDGES' COMMENTS THE STUDENT ACCOUNT HAS A COMPLEX LIST OF FEATURES, WHICH ARE DIFFICULT TO GET ACROSS WITH IMPACT. WHILST NO ONE CAME UP WITH A COMPLETE ANSWER TO THE BRIEF (WHICH WAS ADMITTEDLY QUITE HARD), THE COMMENDED WORK WAS IMAGINATIVE AND QUITE FUNNY, COMBINING A LATERAL TAKE ON THE BRIEF WITH AN ENCOURAGING DEGREE OF CRAFT SKILL ON DISPLAY IN THE EXECUTIONS. **NICK MOORE**

THE ENTRANTS SHOULD HAVE KNOWN MORE ABOUT STUDENT LIFE THAN ME… THERE WERE TOO MANY VISUAL CLICHÉS AND TOO MANY HIGHLY FINISHED FIRST THOUGHTS. BUT THEN I'M OLD, SO MAYBE I JUST DIDN'T UNDERSTAND ANY OF IT. **NIGEL EDGINTON-VIGUS**

I WONDER HOW THE STUDENTS WOULD HAVE REACTED IF WE HAD ADDRESSED THEM WITH THEIR OWN IDEAS? THEY ARE THE TARGET AUDIENCE AFTER ALL. I'M SURE THEY COULD HAVE BROUGHT SO MUCH MORE TO THE PARTY. ALSO, AS A GENERAL COMMENT CONSIDERING THE CATEGORY, IDEAS FOR RESPONSE MECHANISMS WERE GENERALLY ABSENT AMONGST THE ENTRIES. **ALEXA CRANER**

Darren Hughes
NatWest

Alexa Craner
TBWA\GGT

Nigel Edginton-Vigus
TBWA\GGT

Nick Moore
TBWA\GGT

Holly Acland
Marketing Direct

Commendation

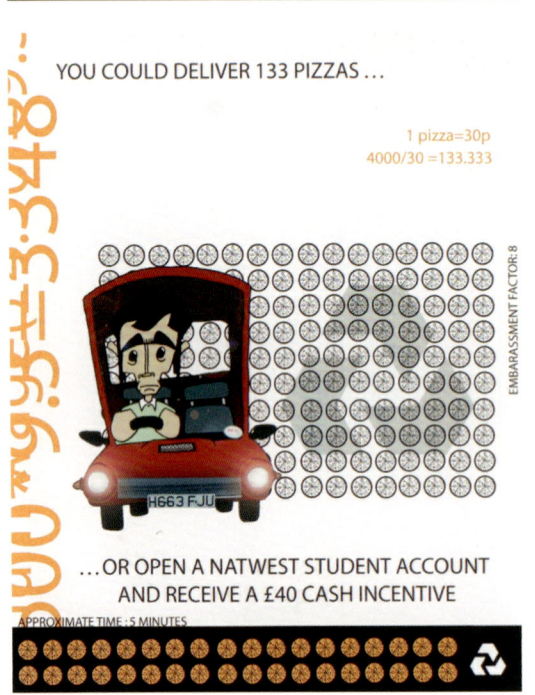

Student
Simon Newman

Tutors
Mike Kelly
Ron Mitchell

College
Newcastle Under Lyme College

YOU COULD WASH 3348 DISHES…

£40/minimum wage(£4.30)=9.3hours
1 dish =10 seconds
*6*6=600*9.3=3348

EMBARASSMENT FACTOR: 7

…OR OPEN A NATWEST STUDENT ACCOUNT AND RECEIVE A £40 CASH INCENTIVE

APPROXIMATE TIME : 5 MINUTES

YOU COULD CLEAN 112 PUBLIC TOILETS…

£40/minimum wage(£4.30)=9.3hours
1 toilet = 5 minutes *12 = 1 hour
12 * 9.3 = 111.6 (112)

EMBARASSMENT FACTOR: 10

…OR OPEN A NATWEST STUDENT ACCOUNT AND RECEIVE A £40 CASH INCENTIVE

APPROXIMATE TIME : 5 MINUTES

YOU COULD DELIVER 133 PIZZAS…

1 pizza=30p
4000/30 =133.333

EMBARASSMENT FACTOR: 8

…OR OPEN A NATWEST STUDENT ACCOUNT AND RECEIVE A £40 CASH INCENTIVE

APPROXIMATE TIME : 5 MINUTES

Commendation

Student
Julia Elton-Bott

Tutor
Blair McLeish

College
Curtin University

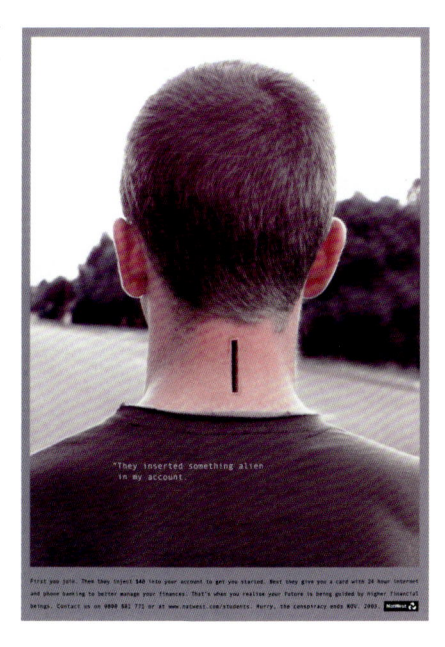

Students
Catherine Etchells
Gemma Pearce
Karen Williamson

Tutors
Frank Holmes
Nick Holmes
Jon Dytor
Dave Sturdy

College
University of Gloucestershire

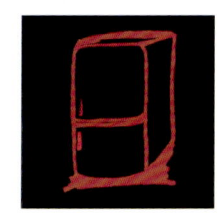

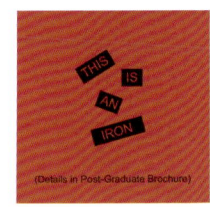

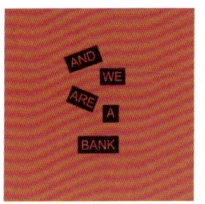

075

School of Graphic Design
BA
GRAPHIC
DESIGN
GEORGE
HADLEY
KINGSTON
YOU GO?
2003

SPONSORED BY
MAK ARCHITECTS

MAK

ENVIRONMENTAL DESIGN

THE BRIEF DESIGN A HOUSE FOR THE FUTURE, WHICH IS A UNIQUE AND ENJOYABLE EXPERIENCE WHILST BEING A PRACTICAL AND REALISTIC SOLUTION TO THE CONTEMPORARY PROBLEMS OF URBAN LIVING. THE DESIGN OF THE HOME SHOULD BE EASILY TRANSPORTABLE BY ROAD OR RAIL AND BE ACCOMPANIED BY PROMOTIONAL MATERIAL, WHICH PICTURES THE HOME IN A SPECIFIC LOCATION.

JUDGES' COMMENTS THERE WAS A COMPLETELY DIFFERENT LEVEL OF THINKING GOING ON WITH THE WINNER. THE STUDENT HAD REALLY WORKED OUT HOW THE SCHEME WOULD RELATE TO THE CITY. **GRANT GIBSON**

OF THE DIFFERENT ANSWERS TO THE BRIEF, WHETHER FOCUSSING ON THE MODULAR SYSTEM, ENVIRONMENT OR TRANSPORTATION, MANY THEMES EMERGED THAT WERE INTERESTING AND ORIGINAL… WHILST OTHERS WERE COMPLETELY MAD! **MEREDITH BENNION**

THE WINNING ENTRY WAS AN INSPIRING IDEA THAT YOU COULD REALLY IMAGINE BEING BUILT… **SIMON WOODROFFE**

THERE WAS A CLEAR AND OUTRIGHT WINNER… A FRESH IDEA THAT WORKED ON MANY LEVELS. THIS WAS AN URBAN SOLUTION THAT ALSO WORKED FOR THE STYLE OF THE USER. **STEPHEN SINCLAIR**

HOUSING IS AN ETERNALLY CHALLENGING AREA, AND I WAS LOOKING FOR A PRACTICAL YET RADICAL IDEA TO SUCCESSFULLY ANSWER THE BRIEF. **THOMAS HEATHERWICK**

Grant Gibson
Blueprint

Thomas Heatherwick
Thomas Heatherwick Studio

Ken Mackay
MAK Architects

Meredith Bennion
MAK Architects

Simon Woodroffe
YO! Sushi

Stephen Sinclair
MAK Architects

First

Student
Jamie Sage

Tutor
Geoffrey Thomas-Shaw

College
Chelsea College
of Art and Design

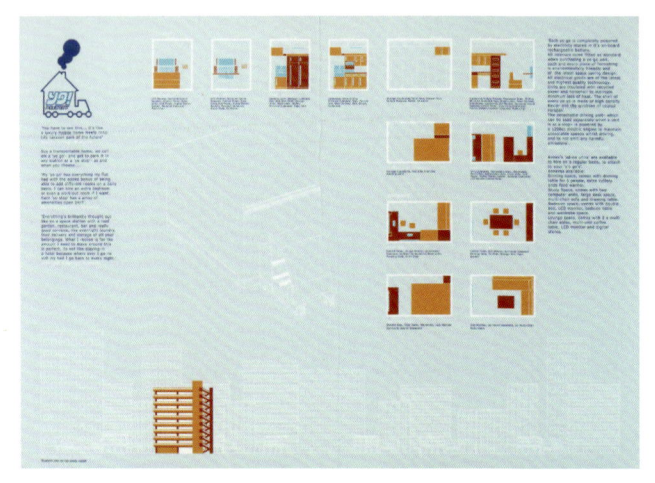

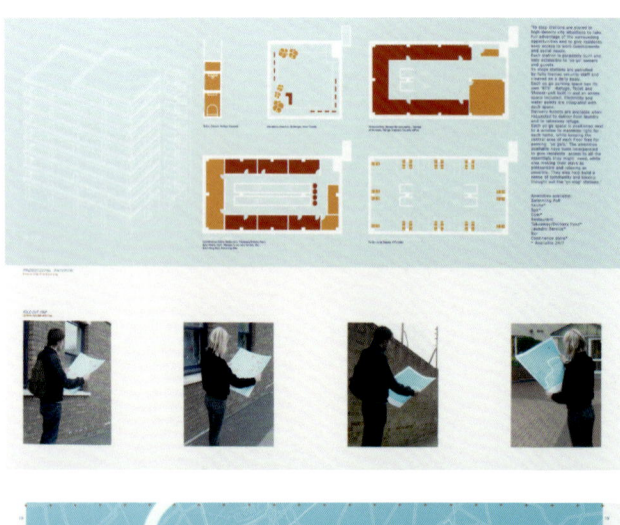

078

Commendation

Student
Catherine Nippe

Tutors
Simon Clarke
Joachim Hetzel
Jon Hares

College
University of Portsmouth

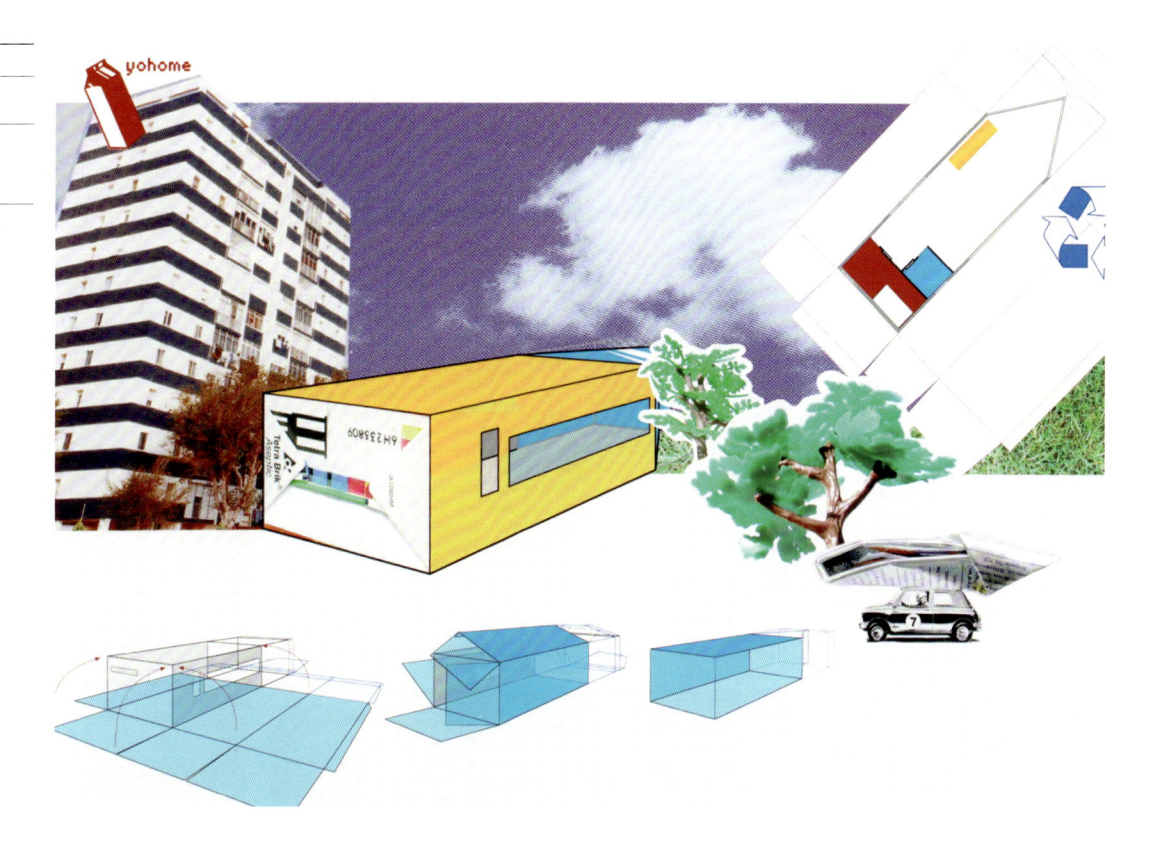

Student
Stephan Roux

Tutor
Nigel Robinson

College
Buckinghamshire Chilterns
University College

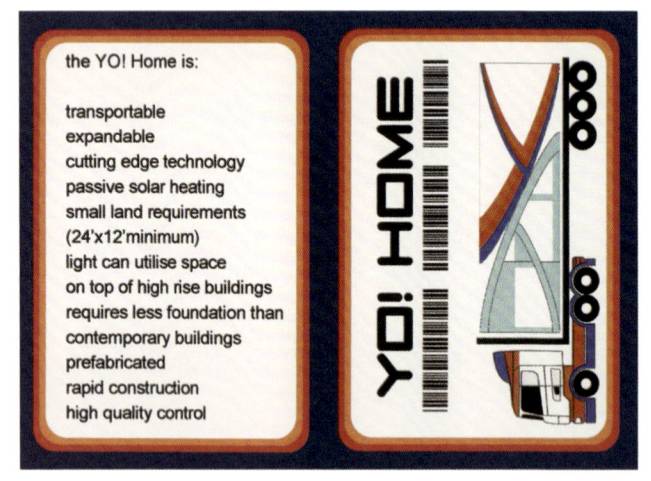

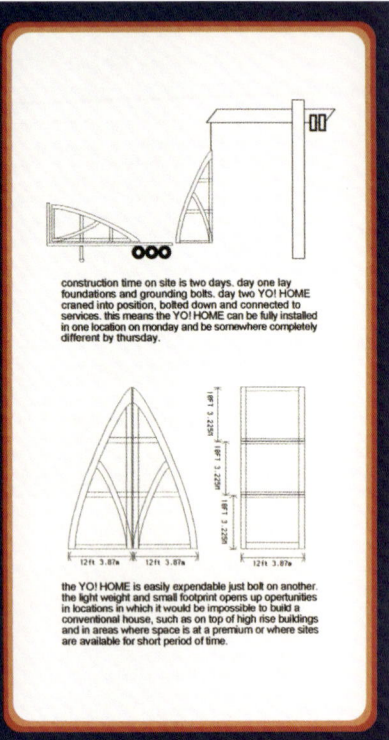

A COMPLETE YO! HOME

construction time on site is two days. day one lay foundations and grounding bolts. day two YO! HOME craned into position, bolted down and connected to services. this means the YO! HOME can be fully installed in one location on monday and be somewhere completely different by thursday.

the YO! HOME is easily expendable just bolt on another. the light weight and small footprint opens up opertunities in locations in which it would be impossible to build a conventional house, such as on top of high rise buildings and in areas where space is at a premium or where sites are available for short period of time.

the YO! Home is:

transportable
expandable
cutting edge technology
passive solar heating
small land requirements
(24'x12'minimum)
light can utilise space
on top of high rise buildings
requires less foundation than
contemporary buildings
prefabricated
rapid construction
high quality control

YO! HOME

Student
Roderick McLachlan

Tutors
Bjorn Rodnes
Andrew Gliddens

College
Napier University

Nick Meakins
HNC Graphic Design
Oxford College of Further Education

SPONSORED BY ADOBE

GRAPHIC DESIGN

THE BRIEF CREATE AN IMMEDIATE IMPACT CAMPAIGN THAT INTRODUCES ADOBE ACROBAT TO THE FINANCE, GOVERNMENT OR MANUFACTURING INDUSTRIES. BE IMAGINATIVE, BUT ABOVE ALL FOCUS ON POSITIONING ADOBE AS A TRUSTED PROVIDER OF MISSION-CRITICAL APPLICATIONS SOFTWARE AND DOCUMENT MANAGEMENT SOLUTIONS.

JUDGES' COMMENTS A TOUGH-AS-HELL, REAL LIFE BRIEF WHICH NEEDED THE ENTRANTS TO UNDERSTAND THE PRODUCT AND THE AUDIENCE INTIMATELY… THE SUCCESSFUL ONES WERE THOSE THAT GRASPED THE CHALLENGE FROM A CONCEPTUAL STANDPOINT, AND THEN USED DESIGN TO DRIVE THEIR COMMUNICATION. **JAY BALL**

I WAS ESPECIALLY PLEASED WITH THE CAMPAIGNS THAT DEMONSTRATED THE UBIQUITY OF THE PDF STANDARD FOR COMMUNICATING WITH EVERYONE. HOWEVER, THE WINNER DEMONSTRATED A DEEP UNDERSTANDING OF THE CHALLENGE AND DELIVERED A CAMPAIGN THAT COULD BE USED RIGHT OUT OF THE BOX. IT HAD THE BEST BLEND OF VISUAL AND CUSTOMER MESSAGING THAT MADE IT THE MOST COMPLETE ENTRY. **MARK WHEELER**

I WAS LOOKING FOR AN UNDERSTANDING OF THE TARGET AUDIENCE, AN ABILITY TO PUT THE MESSAGE ACROSS WITH STYLE, WIT AND CONVICTION – TO PUSH AN IDEA AS FAR AS POSSIBLE. THE WINNING ENTRY DIDN'T SHY AWAY FROM USING THE BRAND AND HAD THE ABILITY TO VISUALISE ABSTRACT CONCEPTS IN A FRESH AND SIMPLE WAY. WELL THOUGHT OUT AND WELL EXECUTED. **CAROLINE ROBERTS**

Ranjit Matharu
Adobe

Caroline Roberts
Grafik

Jim Northover
Citygate Lloyd Northover

Jay Ball
Banner Corporation

Gillian Thomas
The Partners

Mark Wheeler
Adobe

First

Student
Taikee Chan

Tutors
Lilian Lindblom-Smith
Geoff Haddon

College
Middlesex University

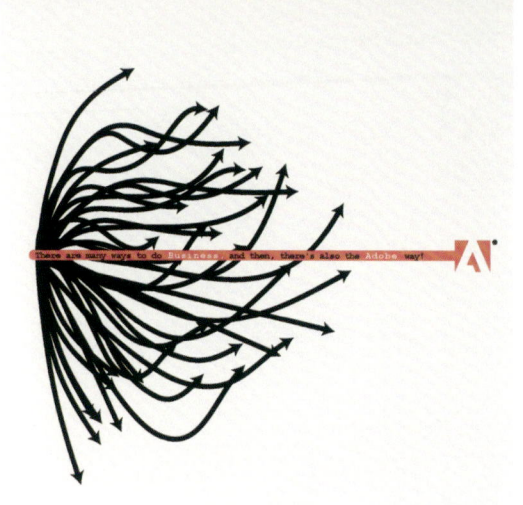

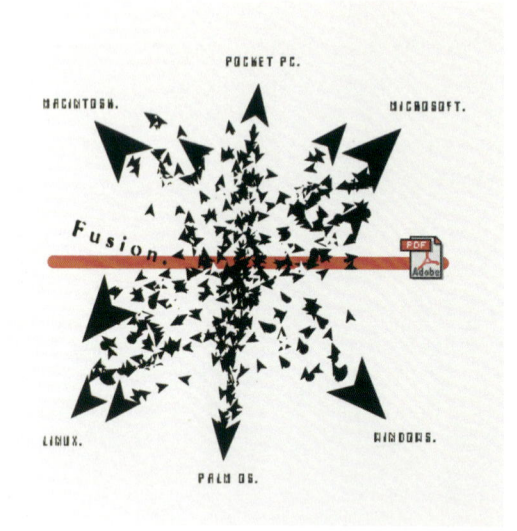

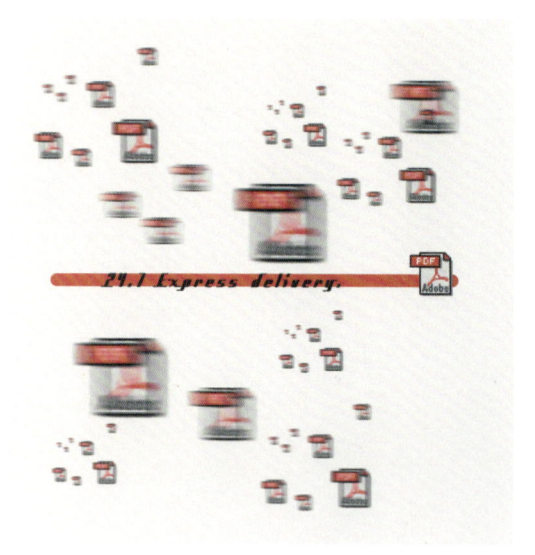

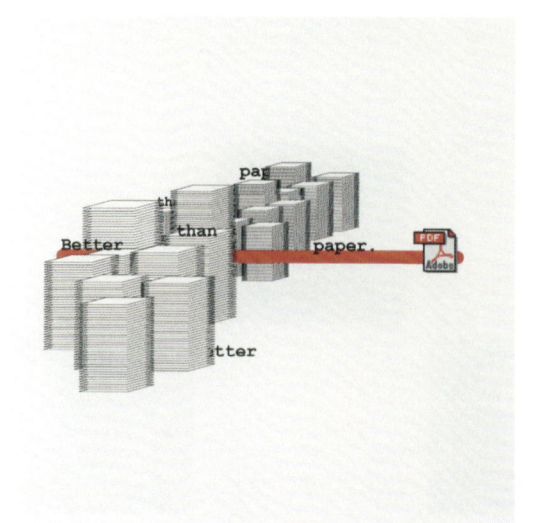

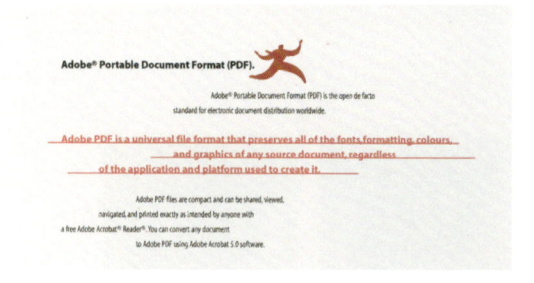

Commendation

Student
Neil Watts

Tutors
Barry Wenden
Paul Wilson
John Holt

College
University College
Northampton

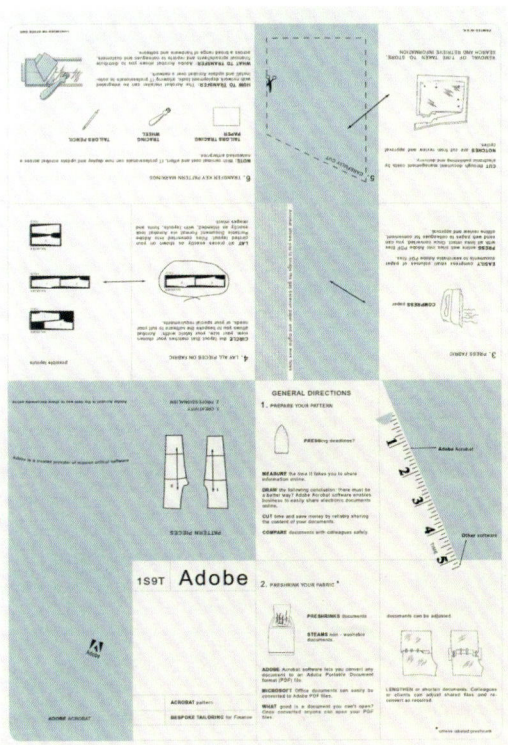

Commendation

Student
Greg Wharton

Tutors
Andy Bainbridge
Jane Souyave
Ron Bray
Tom Shaughnessy

College
University of Central Lancashire

If you are suffering from these symptoms we have the cure for you, 'Adobe Acrobat'. With Acrobat you will completely change the way you work, making life easier, paperwork quicker and cost effective at the same time. This software program will totally revolutionise the way in which you work; streamlining your business and launching it into the twenty first century.

In todays markets brand identity is paramount to a company Acrobat allows you to capture your companies identity digitally so all the documents you send retain that identity. It is exactly the same as sending a letter on headed paper only easier as it is typed straight on the computer and e-mailed to the recipient. When the file is opened the brand identity is preserved and can not be altered

X-RAY

Student
Sam Luk

Tutors
Andy Bainbridge
Pete Thompson

College
University of Central Lancashire

The Sun Shines down on ferret land where there is no WAR!
ferrets Porn Star.
CRAZY!
a crazy ferret.
I Gel
ferrit Lake
worm ferret
ferret formally known as 'Ferret'
A ferrets Home
by John Nielsen
Lizzy & Nat
Harrard Seaton

SPONSORED BY BLOOMBERG

Bloomberg

ILLUSTRATION

THE BRIEF CREATE A PROMINENT AND CONTEMPORARY ILLUSTRATION FOR EXHIBITION IN THE INTERNATIONAL OFFICES OF BLOOMBERG, TO SUIT A WIDE RANGE OF ARCHITECTURALLY DESIGNED SPACES. IDEAS SHOULD ILLUSTRATE BLOOMBERG'S POSITION AS A GLOBAL NEWS AND INFORMATION COMPANY.

JUDGES' COMMENTS THE BRIEF ENCOURAGED ILLUSTRATION TO HOLD ITS OWN IN AN ALREADY HEAVILY STIMULATED ENVIRONMENT. THE COMMENDED PIECE WAS CHOSEN BECAUSE IT DEMONSTRATED EXCELLENT ILLUSTRATION WITH A FRESH, ALTERNATIVE AND PROVOCATIVE RESPONSE TO THE BRIEF. **JEMMA READ**

AS STUDENTS, YOU CAN AFFORD TO RESPOND TO A BRIEF RATHER THAN TO MERELY ANSWER IT, AS IN THE CASE OF THE COMMENDED WORK HERE, WHICH DIDN'T FOLLOW AN OBVIOUS ROUTE. **DEBORAH BEE**

OVERALL, THE RESPONSE WAS QUITE PREDICTABLE. THE WORK WHICH APPEALED TO ME CHALLENGED THE BRIEF WITH A SENSE OF IRONY AND WIT. **MARINA WILLER**

WE WERE LOOKING FOR SOMETHING UNEXPECTED. THERE WAS NO WINNER SIMPLY BECAUSE NOTHING JUMPED OUT. THE ENTRIES SHOULD HAVE BEEN MORE ADVENTUROUS, WHICH THE COMMENDATION WAS – A GOOD HONEST REACTION TO A VERY COMPLEX COMPANY AND BRIEF. **JOHNNY HANNAH**

Johnny Hannah
Illustrator

Marina Willer
Wolff Olins

William Webb
Bloomsbury Publishing

Deborah Bee
Editor

Jemma Read
Bloomberg

Commendation

Student
Cheynne Edmonston

Tutors
Robert Shadbolt
Nancy Slonims
Geoff Grandfield

College
Middlesex University

Bollocks   Bloomberg

EARN   LIVE?

CULTURE    CAPITALISM

ARSE

PROFIT

Student
Vicki Lau

Tutor
Christine McCauley

College
University of Westminster

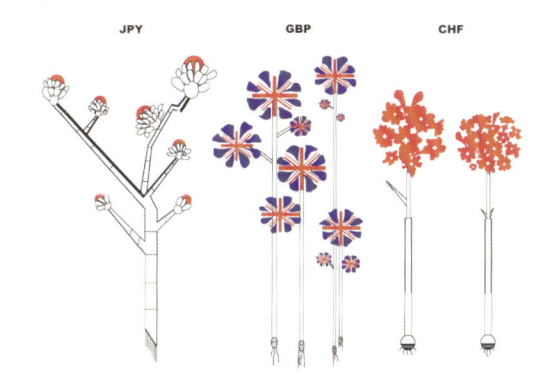

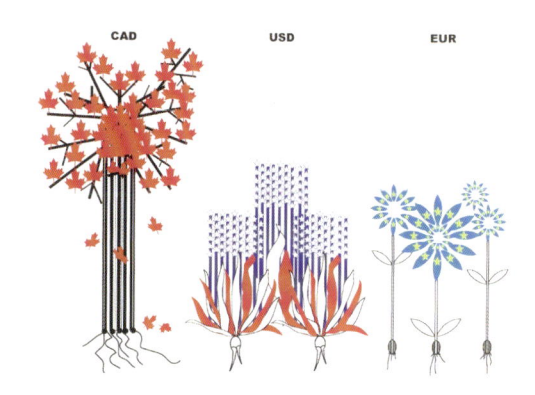

Students
Ottilia Aviram
Chi Van Nim

Tutors
Derek Yates
Elliot Thoburn
Charlotte Oelerich

College
Southwark College

Student
Morton Moerland

Tutors
Andrew Baker
Bren Nevin
Bev Whitehead

College
Surrey Institute of Art and Design University College at Epsom

Students
Martin Norrlind
Linus Ostberg

Tutors
Peter Viksten
Dennis Dahlqvist

College
Forsbergs School of Graphic Design and Advertising

Student
Asa Lucander

Tutors
Robert Shadbolt
Nancy Slonims
Geoff Grandfield

College
Middlesex University

Student
Clive Nicholson

Tutor
Brian Love

College
Kingston University

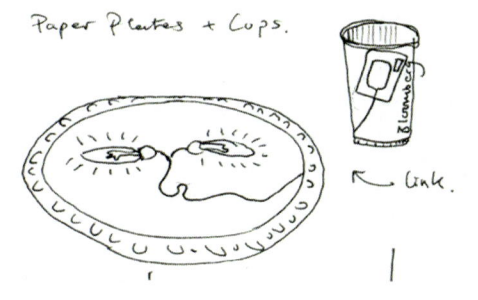

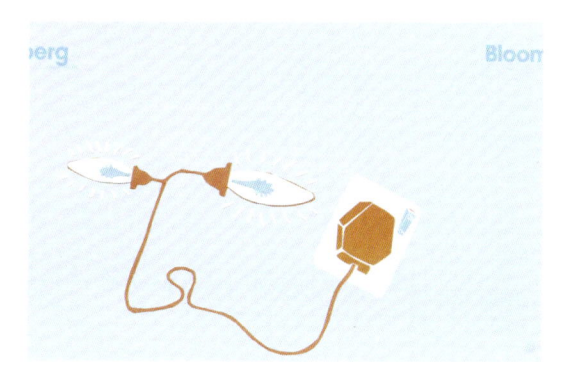

NIA

SPONSORED BY
DEPARTMENT OF HEALTH,
DESIGN COUNCIL AND NATIONAL
PATIENT SAFETY AGENCY

NHS

Design Council

NHS
National Patient Safety Agency

INFORMATION DESIGN

THE BRIEF DESIGN A FUNDAMENTAL IMPROVEMENT IN THE WAY INFORMATION FOR A FAMILIAR MEDICATION IS COMMUNICATED TO ENHANCE ITS SAFE USE. DESIGN CAN BE A MATTER OF LIFE AND DEATH IN THE HEALTH SERVICE AND IDEAS SHOULD DISPLAY A STRONG CONNECTION BETWEEN USER INSIGHT AND INNOVATIVE DESIGN SOLUTIONS.

JUDGES' COMMENTS THIS WAS A CHALLENGING BRIEF IN AN IMPORTANT AREA, WHERE GOOD DESIGN REALLY CAN MAKE A DIFFERENCE. THE OVERALL STANDARD OF THE WORK WAS GENERALLY GOOD, BUT WITH THE WINNING ENTRY THE RESEARCH WAS EVIDENT AND THE CONCEPT DEVELOPED WITH REAL USER FOCUS. THE DESIGN WAS FULLY DEVELOPED WHILST ADDRESSING A COMPLEX NEED FOR BOTH INFORMATION AND A SYSTEM OF CONTROL, MAKING THE MEDICATION BOTH EASIER AND SAFER TO USE. A GREAT SOLUTION, VERY WELL COMMUNICATED. **LESLEY MORRIS**

THIS IS PROBABLY THE MOST DIFFICULT AREA TO DEVELOP NEW IDEAS BECAUSE OF THE VERY COMPLEX NATURE OF THE PRODUCTS – FOR EXAMPLE, 'GET THE INFORMATION WRONG AND PEOPLE WILL DIE'. IT IS GREAT TO SEE STUDENTS PREPARED TO ANSWER SUCH A DIFFICULT BRIEF… THE TRICK WAS TO HELP NOT HINDER IN THE SOLUTION. **SIMON JOHN**

MANY ENTRIES LOOKED MORE CONFUSED AND COMPLEX THAN THE ORIGINAL MEDICINES THEY WERE CREATING A SOLUTION FOR, WHICH IN FACT HELPED HIGHLIGHT THE STRENGTHS OF THE WINNER EVEN FURTHER… **LUKE GIFFORD**

Simon John
Ergo-ID

Helen Glenister
National Patient
Safety Agency

Luke Gifford
Johnson Banks

Lesley Morris
Design Council

David Knight
Department
of Health

First

Student
Debbie McKay

Tutors
David Herbert
Gordon Robertson

College
Duncan of Jordanstone
College of Art

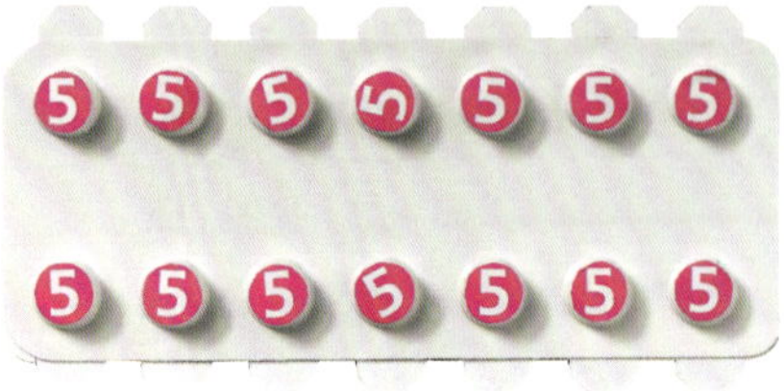

096

Second

Student
Adam Bates

Tutors
Les Porter
Michelle Douglas

College
Brunel University

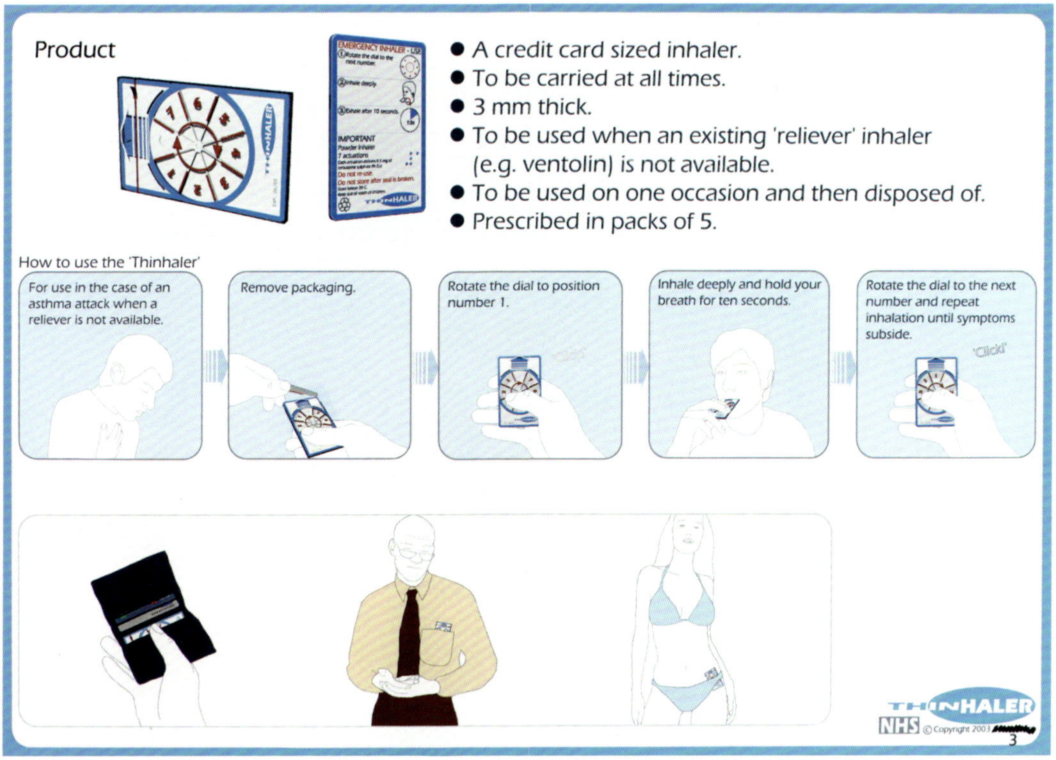

Product

- A credit card sized inhaler.
- To be carried at all times.
- 3 mm thick.
- To be used when an existing 'reliever' inhaler (e.g. ventolin) is not available.
- To be used on one occasion and then disposed of.
- Prescribed in packs of 5.

How to use the 'Thinhaler'

1. For use in the case of an asthma attack when a reliever is not available.
2. Remove packaging.
3. Rotate the dial to position number 1.
4. Inhale deeply and hold your breath for ten seconds.
5. Rotate the dial to the next number and repeat inhalation until symptoms subside. 'Click!'

THINHALER
NHS © Copyright 2003

Commendation

Student
Tomoko Ishii

Tutor
Hazel Rattigan

College
Central Saint Martins/
College of Art and Design

PACKAGING

We tend to lose the instruction of medicine even though they may be important.
Also I normally don't keep the box. I keep the pills on their own.
So I thought I could combine the instructions, box and pills together.
I attached the instruction to the pills and it also has the function of a box.

GRAPHICS

I made the text as big as possible and the line space as big as possible to make the text easier to read.
Each category of information has its own colour and icon.
On the first section, you see the icon with their colour code. You can follow the colour of the section you want to read as you open.

Student
Nina Sletten

Tutors
Clive Colledge
Phil Thomson
David Knight

College
Birmingham Institute
of Art and Design

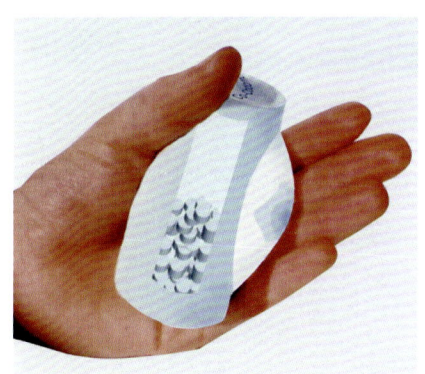

Window to view tablets

tablets comes out here

Students
Nicolas Markwald
Nina Neusitzer

Tutor
Hans-Gunter Schmitz

College
Bergische Universität
Wuppertal

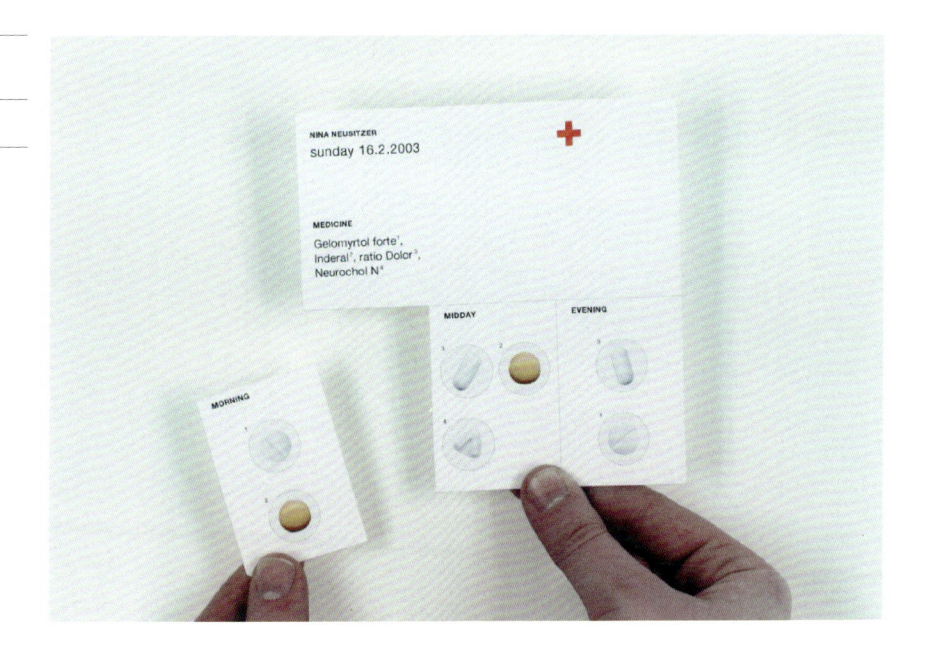

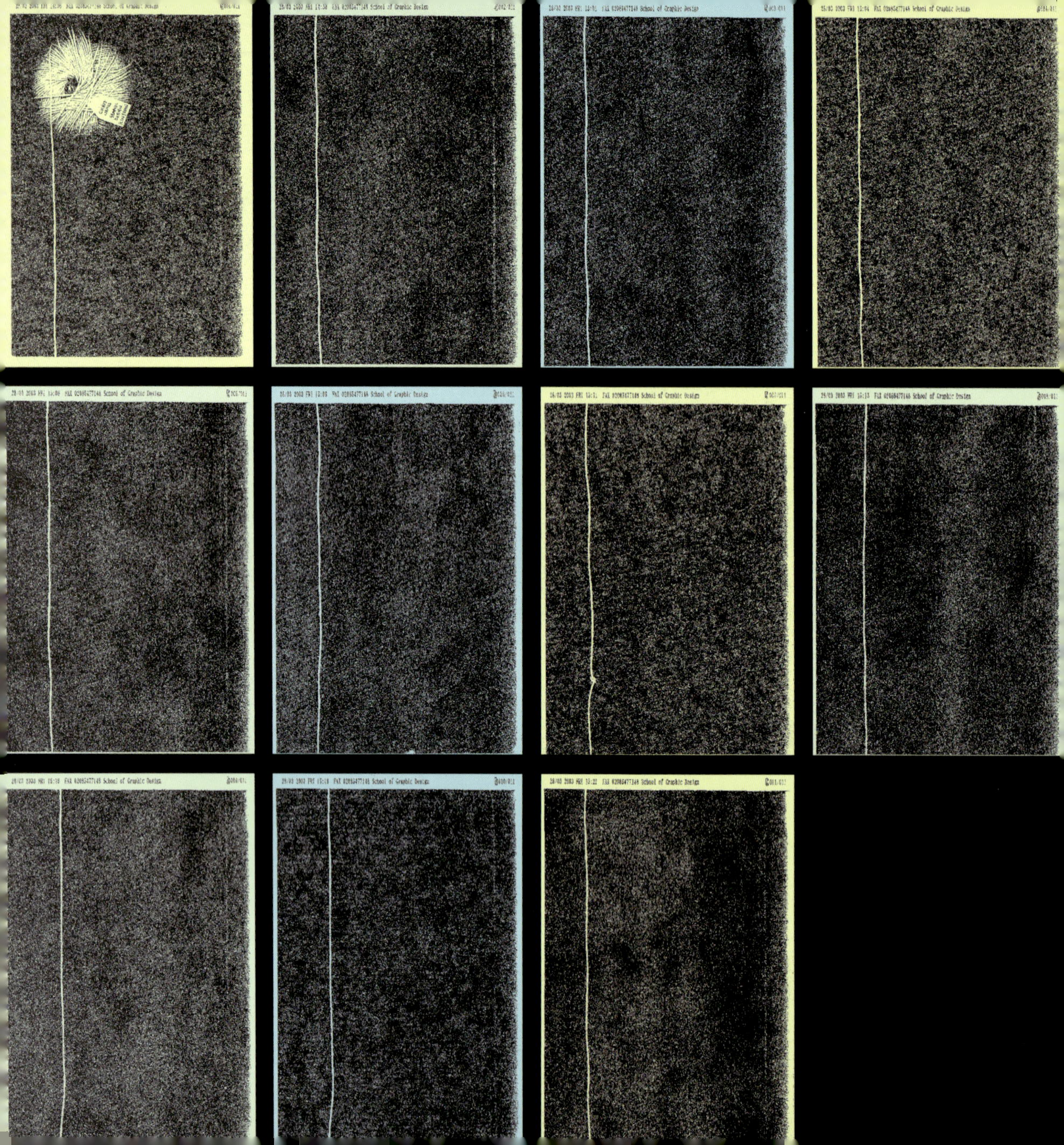

SPONSORED BY
BT

INTERACTIVE DESIGN

THE BRIEF CREATE AND DESIGN ALL THE ASPECTS OF A VIDEO GREETINGS CARDS SHOP, FROM DESIGNING AND MAKING THE VIDEO CARDS TO SHOWING HOW THEY WOULD BE PURCHASED, SELECTED AND CUSTOMISED. THE KEY ELEMENTS OF THE BRIEF ARE THOSE OF DESIGN AND INTERFACE RATHER THAN TECHNOLOGY.

JUDGES' COMMENTS THE WINNER LOOKED BEYOND THE OBVIOUS 'WRITE A CAPTION OVER SOME VIDEO' SOLUTION AND CAME UP WITH NOVEL USES OF ANIMATION. **GORDON BUTLER**

TECHNICAL RESTRAINTS MAY HAVE PREVENTED ENTRANTS FROM REALLY USING THEIR IMAGINATION. THE WINNER LOOKED LIKE THEY'D HAD FUN AND PRODUCED SOMETHING THEY ACTUALLY WANTED TO USE. **VICKY ATKINSON**

A TOUGH BUT EXCITING BRIEF. WHILST THE OVERALL STANDARD OF ENTRY WAS OK, THE WORK WAS MORE CONSERVATIVE THAN I WOULD HAVE LIKED TO HAVE SEEN. **SEBASTIAN ROYCE**

THE WINNER OF THIS YEAR'S AWARD SHOULD ENCOURAGE NEXT YEAR'S ENTRANTS TO TAKE A CREATIVE APPROACH FIRST AND FOREMOST AND NOT FEEL CONSTRAINED BY WHAT THEY FEEL IS EXPECTED OF AN INTERACTIVE BRIEF. **ROB O'CONNOR**

Sebastian Royce
Glue London

Jenny Quillinan
BT

Vicky Atkinson
Computer Arts

Gordon Butler
Fancy a Pint

Rob O'Connor
Stylorouge

Tom Roope
Tomato

First

Student
Tom Rowley

Tutor
Nigel Robinson

College
Buckinghamshire Chilterns University College

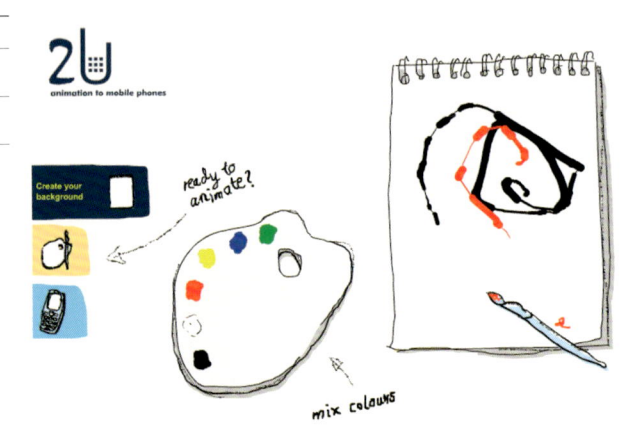

Second

Student
Richard Baxter

Tutors
John Durrant
Andrew McRae

College
Ravensbourne College of Design and Communication

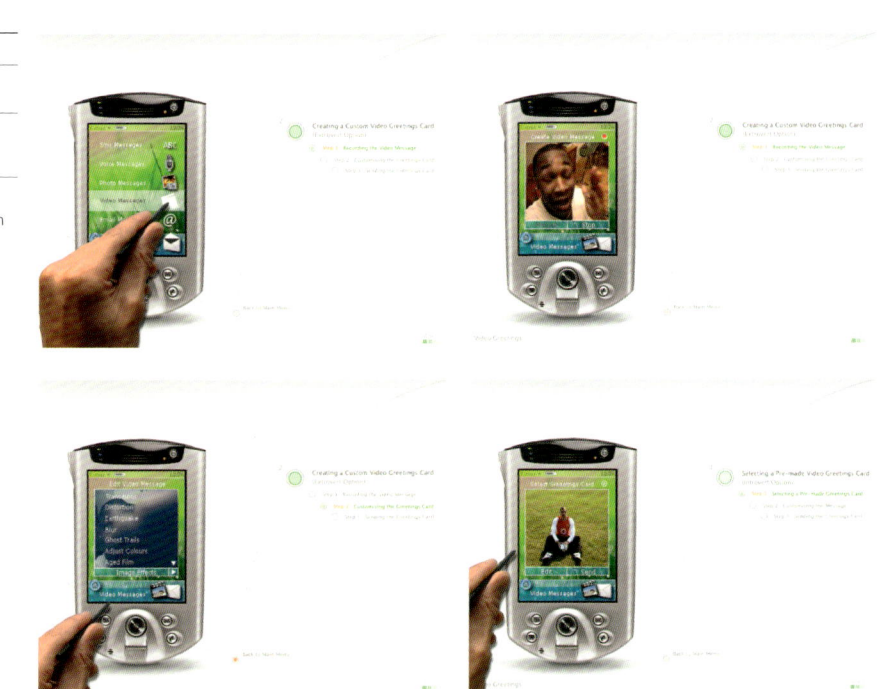

Commendation

Student
Tom Robinson

Tutors
David Gardener
Kate Bonella
Paul Smith
Vicky Isley

College
Southampton Institute

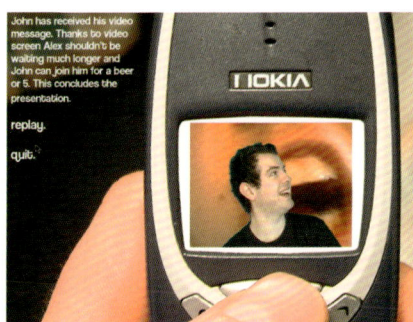

103

RODNEY GRAHAM
VIS COMM.
GLASGOW
SCHOOL
OF ART

SPONSORED BY
CORPORATE EDGE

Corporate **Edge**

MIXED MEDIA

THE BRIEF EUROPE, AS THE THIRD BIGGEST TRADING BLOCK IN THE WORLD, NEEDS A NEW IMAGE AND CAMPAIGN TO COMMUNICATE A DIVERSITY OF MESSAGES. CREATE AN EXCITING, NEW FACE WHICH CONSTITUTES THIS CORE IDEA OF A EUROPEAN BRAND, AND THEN DEMONSTRATE HOW THIS IDENTITY WILL WORK IN EITHER A POSTER, PRINT CAMPAIGN OR WEBSITE.

JUDGES' COMMENTS BRANDING A COUNTRY IS HARD, BUT BRANDING A CONTINENT THAT IS STILL GROWING AND WHERE THERE ARE SO MANY NATIONS AND LANGUAGES IS A BIG, BIG CHALLENGE. I WANTED TO SEE SOMETHING THAT CARRIED EUROPE FORWARD, AND HANDLED THE ISSUE OF IDENTITY WITH BRAVERY AND ORIGINALITY. THE WORK IN BOOK WAS BY FAR THE BEST, BACKED UP WITH EITHER BELIEF OR CREATIVE BRILLIANCE. **STUART DICKINSON**

THE SECOND PRIZE WINNER HAD A STRONG UNDERLYING CONCEPT. IT WAS THE MOST COMPLETE ATTEMPT ON THE BRIEF. IT REFLECTED A DISTINCTLY EUROPEAN STYLE, DELIVERED A THOUGHTFUL MESSAGE AND HAD A SUBTLE YET VIVID OVERALL PERSONALITY AND BRAND STYLE. **CREENAGH LODGE**

WE FELT THAT THE CENTRAL CONCEPT OF THE SECOND PRIZE WINNER RANG TRUE, THE IDEA OF EUROPE BECOMING INGRAINED IN ALL OF US AS WE ASSIMILATED THE VARIOUS ASPECTS OF ITS DIVERSE CULTURE WAS VERY STRONG, WITH ITS EXECUTION VERY ARRESTING. **JENNIE WINHALL**

Creenagh Lodge
Corporate Edge

Emiko Terazona
Financial Times

Stuart Dickinson
Corporate Edge

Cherie Lebbon
HHRC

Jennie Winhall
Design Council

Second

Students
Julia Greiner
Ekaterina Grizik
Yvonne Reuter

Tutors
Charlotte Schröner
Thomas Daum

College
Fachhochschule Mainz

Pay attention to the mark, the mark is the concept.

Europe doesn't need to create an identity, Europe has an identity allready. The unique history, culture and variety of the smallest continent on earth attracts people around the globe and influences other cultures worldwide. Travelling in Europe you gather experiences that ultimately become a part of you, like growing a beautymark.

Commendation

Students
Eva Hoefer
Tanja Jonath-Pieoler
Eric Schmitt

Tutors
Charlotte Schroner
Thomas Daum

College
Fachhochschule Mainz

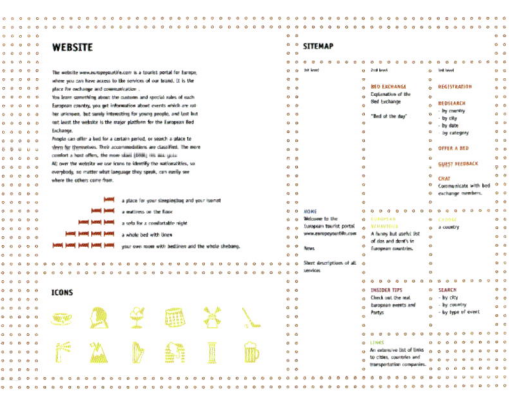

Students
Christine Buhl
Csilla Gyertyanosi
Gregor Von Sievers

Tutors
Charlotte Schroner
Thomas Daum

College
Fachhochschule Mainz

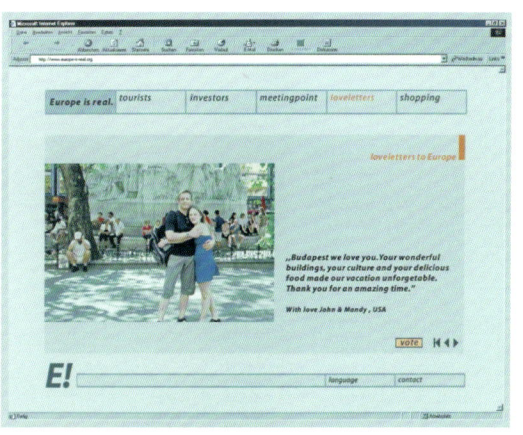

Students
Sebastian Heilig
Till Heim
Robert Schwartz

Tutors
Charlotte Schroner
Thomas Daum

College
Fachhochschule Mainz

Student
Rochus Dahnken

Tutors
Sian Cook
Martin Schooley

College
Ravensbourne College of Design and Communication

Student
Klaire Webster

Tutors
Mike Davidson
Anne Colwell
Mario Minichiello

College
Loughborough University

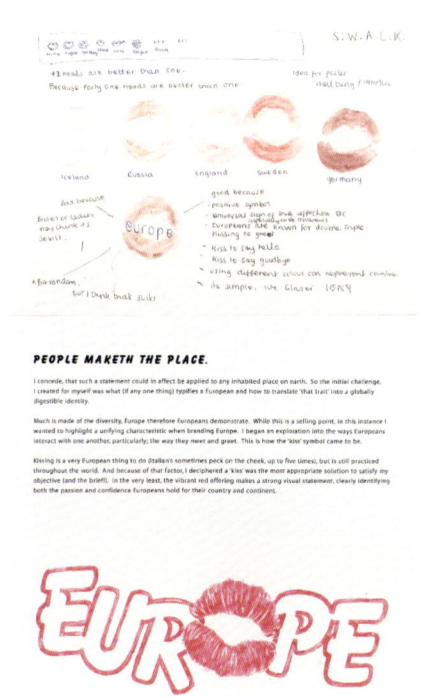

YE GADS!! MY BODY HAS TRANSFORMED BEYOND ALL BELIEF!! FROM THIS DAY FORTH, I SHALL CALL MYSELF
FANTASTIC FERRET

SPONSORED BY NESTA - THE NATIONAL ENDOWMENT FOR SCIENCE, TECHNOLOGY AND THE ARTS, DESIGN COUNCIL, HELEN HAMLYN RESEARCH CENTRE, IDEO, ITC AND CONSUMERS' ASSOCIATION

NESTA PRODUCT DESIGN AND INNOVATION AWARDS

THE BRIEF – DESIGN COUNCIL/HELEN HAMLYN RESEARCH CENTRE DESIGN A NEW OBJECT OBSERVING THE NEEDS OF PARENTS AND CHILDREN, PROVIDING A SOLUTION WHICH IS SAFE, PRACTICAL AND ENJOYABLE.

JUDGE'S COMMENT THE OVERALL WINNER HAD A SIMPLICITY THAT STOOD OUT – A CONCEPT THAT GAVE A ROBUST DESIGN SOLUTION TO A CLEARLY IDENTIFIED USER NEED. **MATT MARSH**

THE BRIEF – IDEO BY EXPLORING WAYS IN WHICH PEOPLE MAKE THE TRANSITION FROM SLEEPING TO WAKING, DESIGN A HANDHELD PERSONAL OBJECT TO ENRICH THIS EXPERIENCE.

JUDGE'S COMMENT THE STRONGEST WORK HAD ADDRESSED REAL LIFE ISSUES AND PROVED THAT THEY HAD ACTUALLY INTERACTED WITH THEIR USERS. MOST ENTRIES WERE NOT STRONG IN COMMUNICATING IDEAS THROUGH PRESENTATION, BUT IT WAS ENCOURAGING TO SEE SO MANY INCORPORATING TANGIBLE ELEMENTS SUCH AS 3D MODELS INTO THEIR DESIGNS AT SUCH AN EARLY STAGE. **INGRID BARON**

THE BRIEF – ITC/CONSUMERS' ASSOCIATION CREATE AN INNOVATIVE CONCEPT TO MAKE INTERACTING WITH DOMESTIC DIGITAL TV EQUIPMENT EASIER FOR EVERYONE.

JUDGES' COMMENT NEARLY EVERY ENTRY TRIED TO MINIMISE THE COMPLEXITIES OF INTERACTING WITH DIGITAL TV – ENCOURAGINGLY MANY DESIGNS WERE FLEXIBLE ENOUGH TO ALLOW NEW FUNCTIONS TO BE ADDED AS THEY APPEAR. **JONATHAN FREEMAN AND MICHELLE CHILDS**

Astrid Zala Jam Design & Communications

Jonathan Knight Fraser Designers

Katrina Koffler Design Council

Irene McAra-McWilliam Royal College of Art

Michelle Childs Consumers' Association

Jeremy Myerson Helen Hamlyn Research Centre

David Hamilton Priestman Goode

Dick Powell Seymour Powell

Jonathan Freeman ITC

Matt Marsh Design Consultant

Ingrid Baron IDEO

Hugo Manassei NESTA

**Products for Parents and Children
Overall Winner**

Student
Nolan Chandler

Tutor
Julian Lindley
Mike Goatman

College
University of Hertfordshire

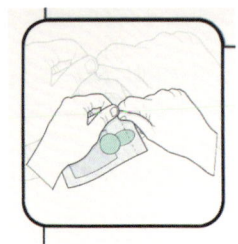

Purchase E.Z.Feed pack.

When ready to use, simply tear off outer sterile packaging and remove E.Z.Feed pack.

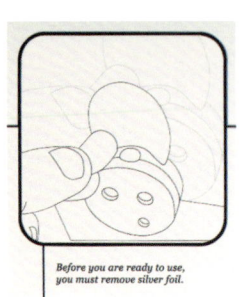

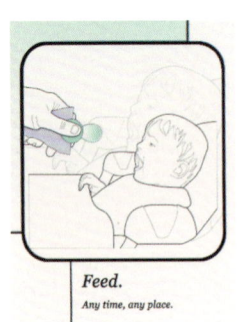

Before you are ready to use, you must remove silver foil.

Feed.

Any time, any place.

Food can be served hot or cold. To heat simply stand in hot water for a few minutes or heat in a microwave.

Microwaves are found at most Garages and Motorway services.

Now E.Z.Feed is ready to use, you squeeze the packet gently until there is enough food on the spoon head,

and you simply continue to,

Squeeze and..

Category Winner

Student
Adrien Rovero

Tutor
Patrick Reymond

College
Ecole Cantonale
D'Art de Lausanne

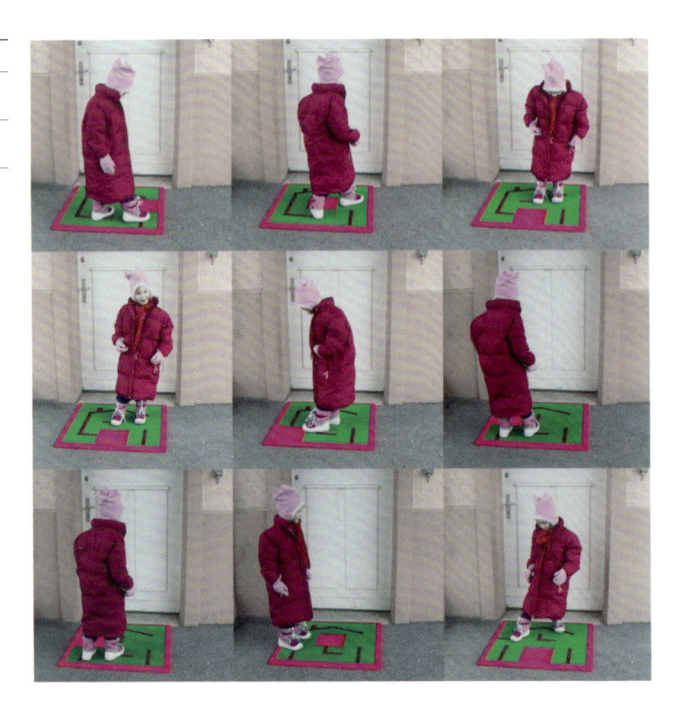

112

Shortlisted

Student
Maya Ishizaki

Tutor
Nick Rhodes

College
Central Saint Martins/
College of Art and Design

Wide opening with two zips on both sides. Single strap offers easy operation.

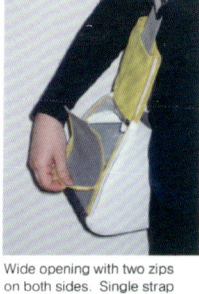

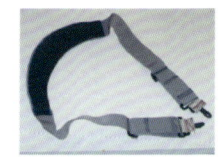

Padded shoulder strap with non-slip material inside. Ergonomic curved shape to reduce strain. Length 90-130cm.

Baby safety strap with extra strong velcro which supports up to 23kg. It is easy to set after putting a baby on the bag.

Extendable key ring fitted.

Side pocket for travelcards.

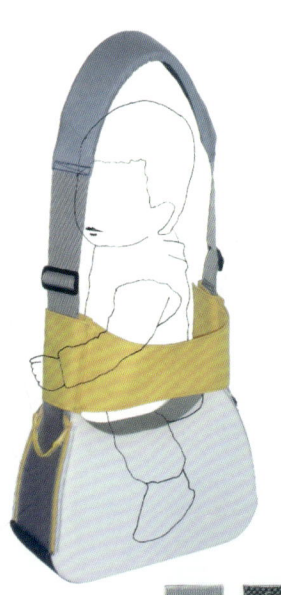

DIMENSION (mm)
Main body : W 320   H 220   D 130

MATERIALS

Body Shell :	High-density Zotefoam laminated with Lycra (vacuum formed)
Side Opening :	Acrylic Canvas (water resistant)
Bottom :	Ballistic Nylon (abrasion resistant)
Safety Strap :	Acrylic Canvas (water resistant)
Webbing :	Nylon
Lining :	PU coated Nylon (water resistant)

Let's go out together

omni BAG

Handheld Object for Sleep Category Winner

Student
Daniel Liden

Tutor
Chris Lefteri

College
Central Saint Martins/ College of Art and Design

YOU ARE 19 TO 40 YEARS OLD. YOU EITHER WORK OR YOU ARE A STUDENT. YOU MAY LIVE WITH YOUR FAMILY OR PARTNER. OR YOU MAY BE LIVING ALONE. YOU SOMETIMES FEEL STRESSED IN YOUR DAY-TO-DAY LIFE. YOU ARE FREQUENTLY HAVING PROBLEMS FALLING ASLEEP. SOMETIMES YOU EITHER WAKE UP TOO SOON OR SEVERAL TIMES DURING THE NIGHT. SOMETIMES YOU HAVE PALPITATIONS.

DO YOU KNOW THAT YOU ARE 3 TIMES AS LIKELY TO DIE BEFORE THE AGE OF 65 IF YOU SUFFER FROM A HIGH RESTING PULSE AND SLEEP DEPRIVATION? DO YOU KNOW THAT THE CHALLENGER, EXXON VALDEZ, BHOPAL & CHERNOBYL CATASTROPHES HAPPENED AS A RESULT OF SLEEP DEPRIVED INDIVIDUALS NOT BEING ABLE TO DO THEIR JOBS PROPERLY?

THIS IS SERIOUS STUFF. LISTEN TO YOUR BODY. SOME PEOPLE WILL BUY PRODUCTS LIKE SLEEPING PILLS AND GIMMICKY LITTLE GADGETS UNDER THE IMPRESSION THAT IT WILL IMPROVE THEIR SLEEP. MY ONLY ADVICE IS THAT YOU TRY AND RESOLVE YOUR PROBLEMS DURING YOUR WAKING HOURS RATHER THAN TRYING TO IMPROVE YOUR SITUATION FROM YOUR ANGST-RIDDEN BED.

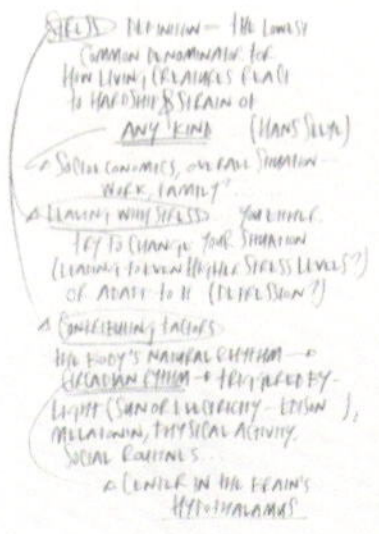

Shortlisted

Student
Anna McManus

Tutors
Paul Rodgers
Ian Lambert
Isla Munro

College
Napier University

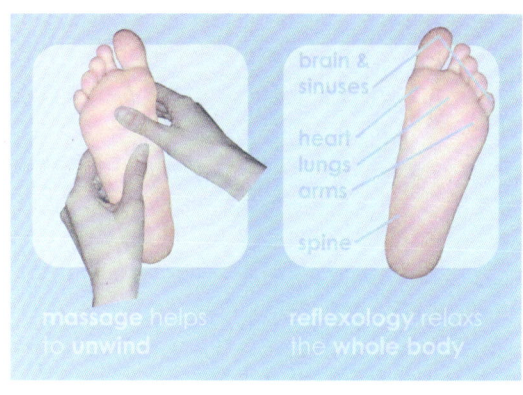

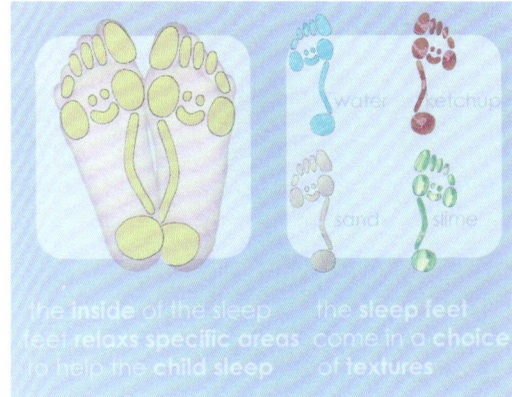

sleep feet

massage helps to **unwind**

reflexology relaxs the **whole body**

the **inside** of the sleep feet relaxs specific areas to help the **child sleep**

the **sleep feet** come in a **choice** of **textures**

Shortlisted

Student
Daniel Bessex

Tutors
Judith Hills
Gerald Emanuel

College
University of Glamorgan

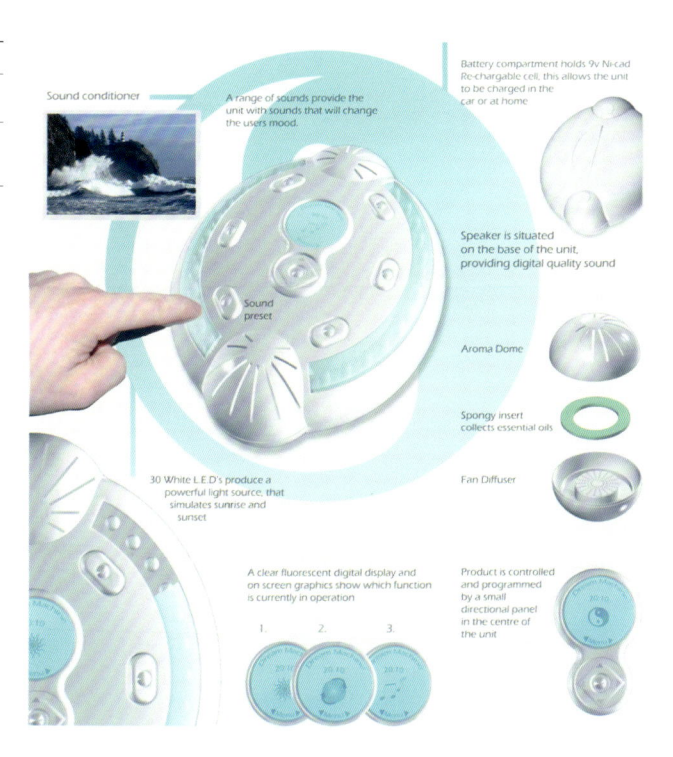

Sound conditioner

A range of sounds provide the unit with sounds that will change the users mood.

Battery compartment holds 9v Ni-cad Re-chargable cell, this allows the unit to be charged in the car or at home

Speaker is situated on the base of the unit, providing digital quality sound

Sound preset

Aroma Dome

Spongy insert collects essential oils

Fan Diffuser

30 White L.E.D's produce a powerful light source, that simulates sunrise and sunset

A clear fluorescent digital display and on screen graphics show which function is currently in operation

Product is controlled and programmed by a small directional panel in the centre of the unit

115

**Interactive Digital TV
Category Winner**

Students
Sarah McCauley
Lisa Tse

Tutors
Ben Hughes
Ralph Ball
Mike Woods

College
Central Saint Martins/
College of Art and Design

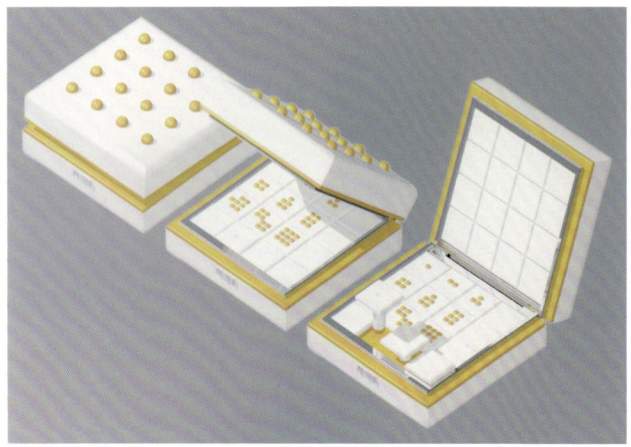

customisable user interface **MiMO**

The MIMO concept has the capacity to make interacting with digital TV easier for a range of users. Mainly, it gives users a sense of comfort with digital TV through tangible physical interaction with objects instead of virtual interfaces.

The arrangement of coloured cubes on the motherboard (MIMO's remote control) reflects the viewing and interaction habits of the user as well as displaying a personalised visual pattern.

Each coloured cube acts as a remote control button; it contains technology which can activate either a specific function, such as volume up or down, or a different digital TV service such as a music channel subscription or web access. When a new function or service is required, the user can add the appropriate cube to the motherboard.

When a cube is activated it is illuminated. Non-active 'dummy' cubes surrounding it contribute a negative spatial element to the composition.

The cubes provide a visual representation of the functions and services available to the user in a range of colours and using a range of icons to be chosen by the user. As each cube fits into every socket, the layout of the motherboard is left entirely up to the user.

As users build their own motherboards they will be aware of the functions of all the cubes they have included. MIMO helps the user most then by only having cubes on the motherboard that the user has chosen to include – to activate functions and services that they actually want and use.

Shortlisted

Student
Ed Stanton

Tutors
Ben Hughes
Ralph Ball
Mike Woods

College
Central Saint Martins/
College of Art and Design

LINK
entertainment manager

MEDIA HUB TO CONTROL DIGITAL TV AND PERIPHERALS IN THE HOME ENVIRONMENT. 01

Shortlisted

Student
Alex Shapowal

Tutors
Paul Rodgers
Alex Milton
Will Titley
Bjorn Rodnes

College
Napier University

TV Guide

To use the TV Guide you must firstly insert your TV Library Card. The card has an inbuilt microchip which allows each user to store and protect their custom choices and preferences.

Content

The TV Guide contains an LCD Touch Screen. When one page is turned and another revealed the screen updates to show the new screen contents. Just like anyother book the pages of the TV Guide can be flicked through and the screen will update quickly, this mirrors the blurring of pages in a book when you flick through it.

The Films and Movies touch screen. Films can be chosen, reviews can be read and adjustments to volume and colour can be made. With the advent of TV On Demand, scheduling will be become unnecessary and you'll be able to watch what you want whenever you want.

Chapter Two   Product

117

I really want to see my face
printed in the D&AD
    Student Awards Annual
    2003

WOULD IT HELP IF I WAS BEAUTIFUL?

SPONSORED BY OLYMPUS

OLYMPUS

PHOTOGRAPHY

THE BRIEF IN THE POST-MODERN WORLD, THE CONCEPT OF NATIONAL IDENTITY HAS BECOME MORE FLUID. AN INDIVIDUAL MAY CHOOSE FROM A PLURALITY OF IDENTITIES, ONLY SOME OF WHICH WILL BE BASED ON THE NATION IN WHICH THEY LIVE. COMMUNICATE THE IDEA OF NATIONAL IDENTITY THROUGH A SERIES OF FOUR TO SIX CHALLENGING IMAGES.

JUDGES' COMMENTS THE HARDEST PART OF THE BRIEF WAS TO AVOID STEREOTYPES. SOME ENTRIES PRESENTED AN INSIGHTFUL VIEW OF NATIONAL IDENTITY BY HIGHLIGHTING ITS SUBTLE INCLUSION IN THE EVERYDAY WHILE CHALLENGING ITS RIGHT TO BE THERE. THE WINNERS STOOD OUT BECAUSE THEY CHALLENGED YOU ON DIFFERENT LEVELS WHILE DRAWING YOU IN AS A VIEWER. **ADAM HINTON**

I WAS HOPING TO SEE SOME POSITIVE REPRESENTATIONS OF NATIONAL IDENTITY, BY CELEBRATING ITS RICHNESS AND DIVERSITY. KNOWING THAT THE BRIEF WAS PERHAPS BETTER SUITED TO REPORTAGE PHOTOGRAPHY, IT DELIGHTED ME TO SEE SOME HAD TRIED ANSWERING IT BY OTHER MEANS INCLUDING STUDIO PHOTOGRAPHY, GRAPHICS AND EVEN FASHION SHOOTS. **RICHARD LANE**

I WANTED TO SEE A HIGHER TECHNICAL STANDARD FROM MANY OF THE ENTRANTS, AND SOME OF THE WORK WAS LET DOWN BY POOR EDITING OR PRESENTATION. THAT ASIDE, THE WINNERS WERE EXCELLENT. CHALLENGING, WELL PHOTOGRAPHED ORIGINAL IMAGES THAT REQUIRED NOTHING MORE THAN VISUAL IMPACT TO SUCCESSFULLY COMMUNICATE THE BRIEF. **DAVE HENDLEY**

Adam Hinton
Photographer

Richard Lane
Olympus

Dave Hendley
Photographer

First

Student
Paul-Michael Berwise-Ebanks

Tutors
Derek Yates
Elliot Thoburn
Charlotte Oelerich

College
Southwark College

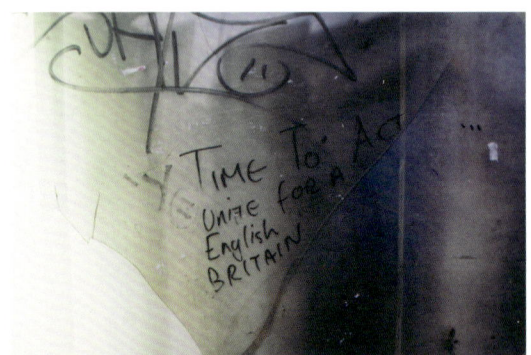

First

Student
Azza Mohamed Suliman

Tutors
John Lowe
Paul Lander
Martyn Hill

College
Birmingham Institute
of Art and Design

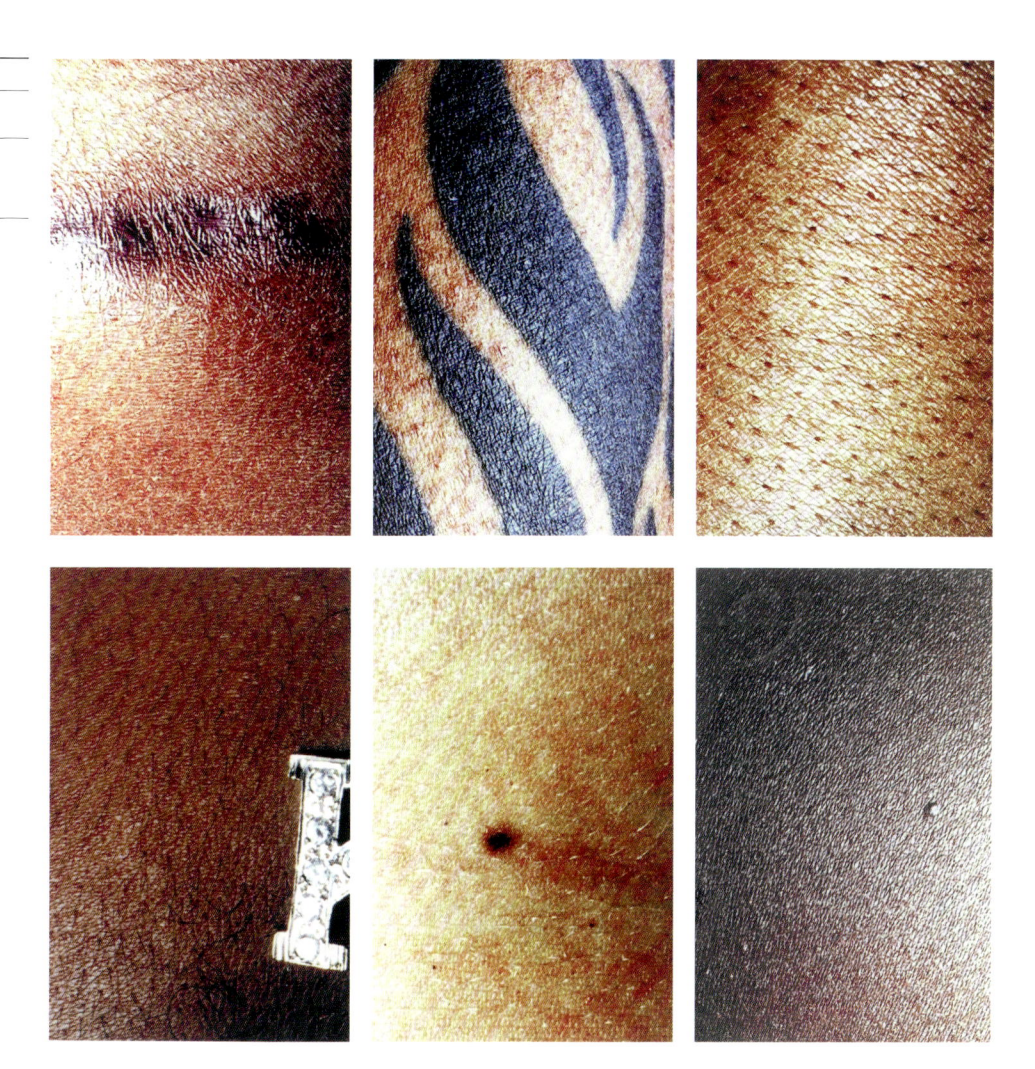

Students
Daniel Baer
Mikael Friden

Tutor
Cath Caldwell

College
Central Saint Martins/
College of Art and Design

Student
James Hughes

Tutor
Kevin Harley

College
University of Central England

Students
Alison Ching
Basia Paczesna
Keshni Sharma

Tutors
John Ingledew
Cath Caldwell
Geoff Fowle

College
Central Saint Martins/
College of Art and Design

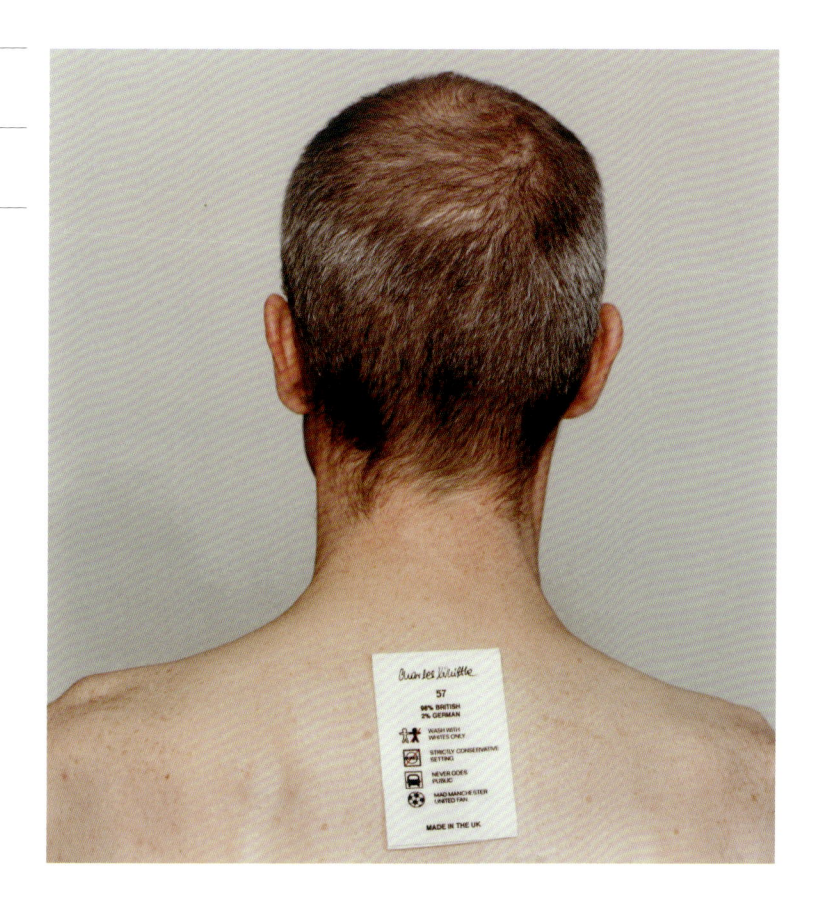

Student
Emma Hunt

Tutors
Karla Newell
Andrew Sides

College
Central Saint Martins/
College of Art and Design

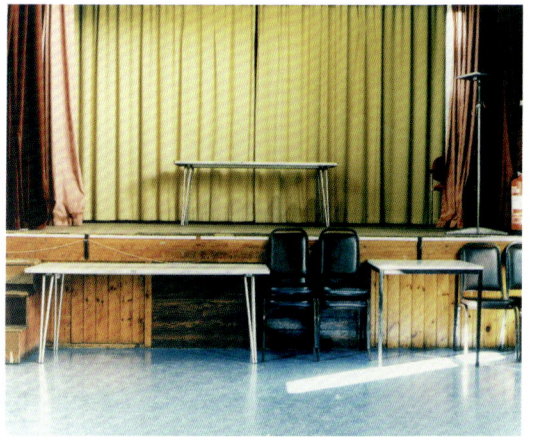

Student
Julia Greisbach

Tutor
Geoffrey Thomas-Shaw

College
Chelsea College
of Art and Design

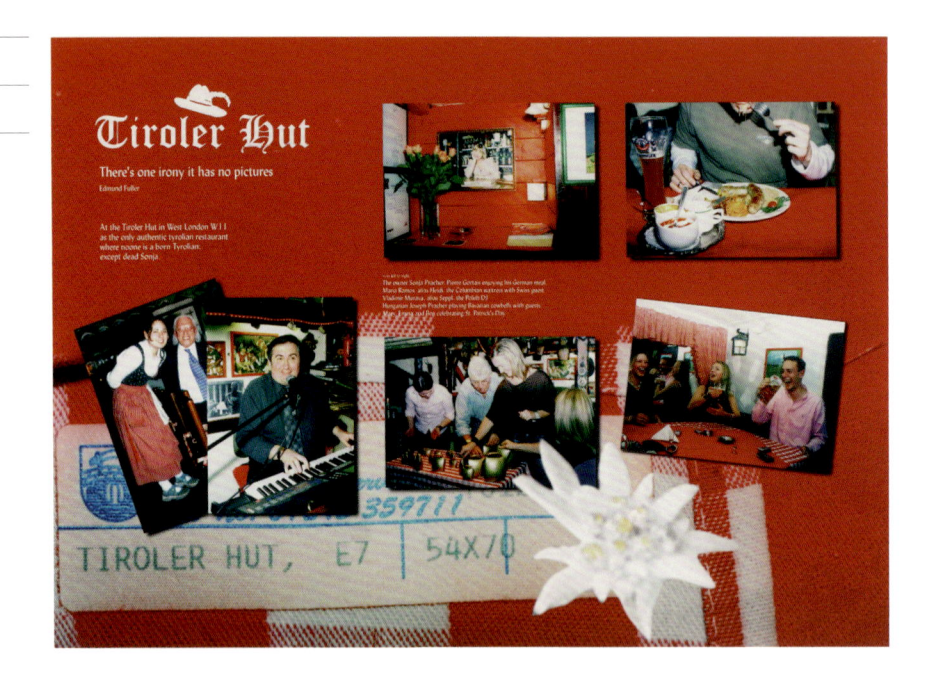

Student
Paul Whidbourne

Tutors
Leah Klein
Julie Wright
John Merriman

College
Buckinghamshire Chilterns
University College

Student
Joss McKinley

Tutor
Steve Harries

College
Central Saint Martins/
College of Art and Design

YOUR JOB

HUGH JANUS
BA GRAPHIC DESIGN
UNIVERSITY OF EAST LONDON

SPONSORED BY
DEPARTMENT FOR WORK
AND PENSIONS

Images of Disability

POSTER ADVERTISING

THE BRIEF DEVELOP A MODERN AND ATTENTION-GRABBING POSTER CAMPAIGN FOR USE AT UK MUSIC FESTIVALS TO RAISE AWARENESS OF THE NEW DEAL FOR MUSICIANS PROGRAMME, WHILST INCLUDING THE APPROPRIATE AND POSITIVE USE OF IMAGES OF DISABILITY.

JUDGES' COMMENTS THE WINNING ENTRY WAS A CLEVER UNEXPECTED IDEA: DISABLED PEOPLE CAN SEE THE OPPORTUNITIES THAT A CAREER IN MUSIC OFFERS THEM IN A WAY THE FULLY ABLED CANNOT. THE WHOLE PRESENTATION WAS HIGHLY FINISHED – YOU COULD EMPLOY THEM TOMORROW!! AMONG ALL THE TOP ENTRIES THE STANDARD WAS AS HIGH AS WE SEE FROM LEADING AGENCIES.
PETER BUCHANAN

WE WERE LOOKING FOR SIMPLE IDEAS CLEARLY EXECUTED AND COURAGE IN REALLY PUSHING IMAGES OF DISABILITY. THERE WERE MORE CHALLENGING IMAGES OF DISABILITY THAN THE WINNER, BUT THE WINNER HAD A THOUGHT-PROVOKING IDEA AT ITS HEART. **JOHN POORTA**

THE BRIEF WAS PARTICULARLY DIFFICULT AND WHILE MANY STRUGGLED WITH THE RIGHT COMBINATION OF IMAGES AND COPY, SOME VERY MATURE AND CONFIDENT IDEAS EMERGED.
MARK TOLLITT

Aleem Siddique
DWP Marketing

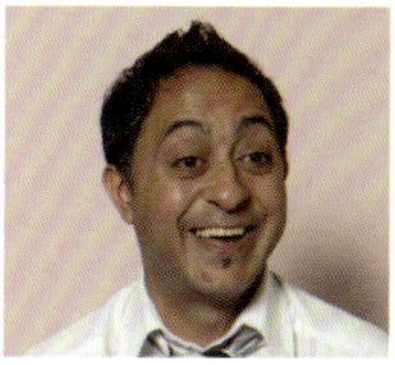

Ben Furner
Furner Communications

Mark Tollitt
DWP Marketing

Peter Buchanan
COI

John Poorta
Leo Burnett

Mike Sutherland
Fallon

Anthony Nelson
Fallon

First

Student
Rihwa Ahn

Tutor
Dominic Dyson

College
London College of Printing

Second

Student
Harinder Bajwa

Tutors
Lin Sinclair
Mike Moran
Mark Lamey

College
University of Central Lancashire

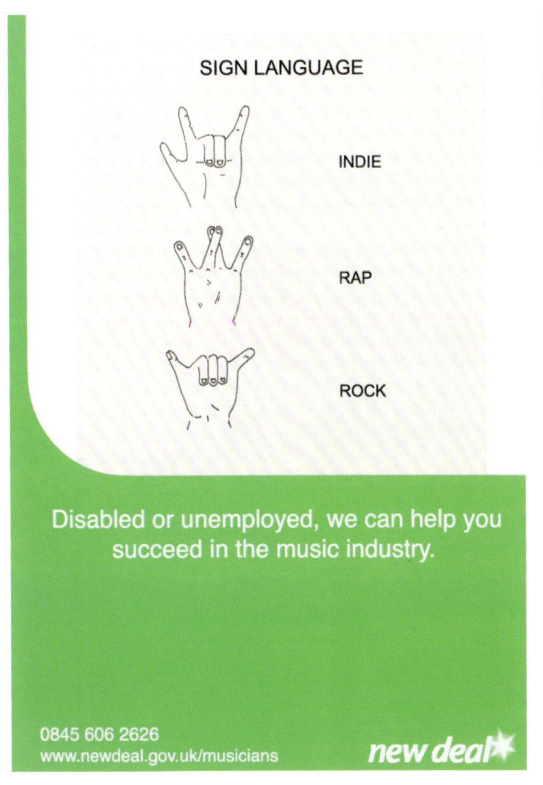

Commendation

Students
Victoria Callister
Pete Richardson

Tutors
Lin Sinclair
Mike Moran
Mark Lamey

College
University of Central Lancashire

129

Students
Paul Kinsella
Cynthia Wong

Tutors
Lin Sinclair
Mike Moran
Mark Lamey

College
University of Central Lancashire

Students
Lesley Coleman
Kim Devall
Lisa Sternberg

Tutors
Norm Grey
Mike Weed

College
The Creative Circus

Students
Lany Jaros
Barbara Tejada

Tutor
Ron Seichrist

College
Miami Ad School

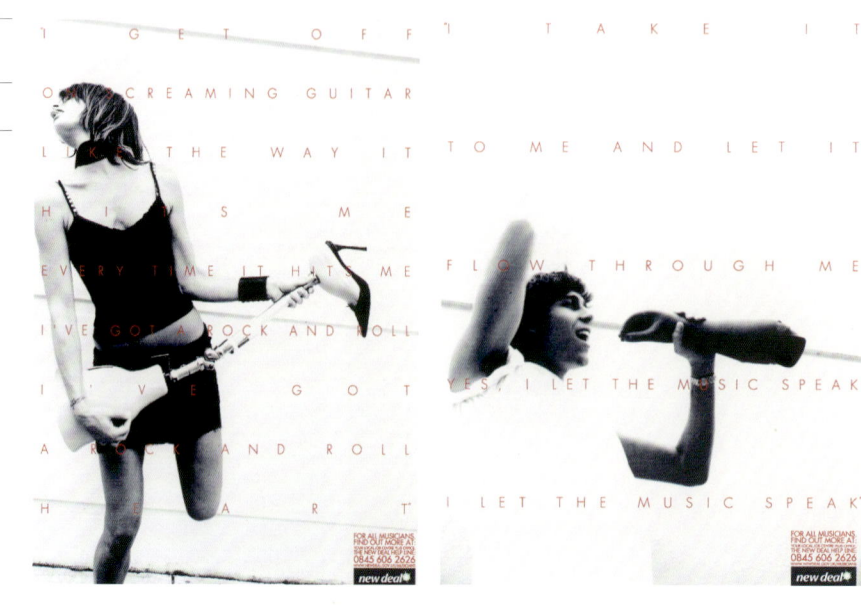

Students
Grey Ingram
Derrick Webb

Tutors
Mark Fensky
Coz Cotzias
Pat Burnham
Charlie Kouns

College
VCU Adcenter

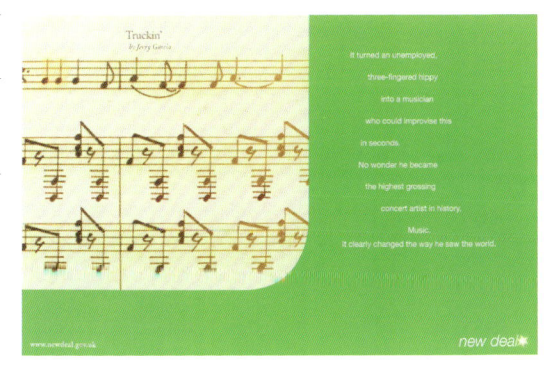

Student
Bruno Tavares

Tutor
Steve Sarson

College
Instituto Politecnico do Porto

Students
Yi Lin Lin
George Primentas

Tutor
Alan Sekers

College
London College of Printing

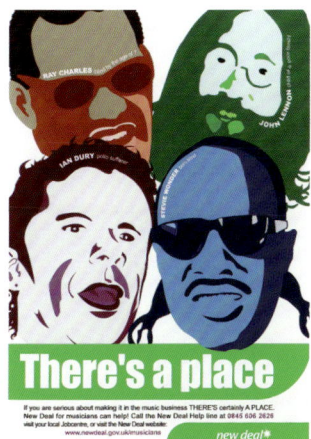

14-JAN-2003 11:54 FROM: 01413534401   TO:9020740790075   P:30/34
james greg, vis com, glasgow school of art.

SPONSORED BY
VIRGIN ATLANTIC

virgin atlantic

PRESS ADVERTISING

THE BRIEF CREATE A PRESS CAMPAIGN LOADED WITH ATTITUDE TO LAUNCH TWO NEW NON-STOP VIRGIN ATLANTIC ROUTES TO GRENADA AND TOBAGO. TO GENERATE A BUZZ AND GET PEOPLE TALKING, THE VISUAL STYLE OF THE CAMPAIGN SHOULD BE IMMEDIATE AND ARRESTING. YOUR CAMPAIGN SHOULD INCORPORATE THE USE OF THE BRAND LOGO AND COLOUR SCHEME, WHILST WORKING IN THE STRIP FORMAT THAT VIRGIN ATLANTIC PIONEERED AS WELL AS MORE TRADITIONAL PRESS FORMATS.

JUDGES' COMMENTS GETTING THE VIRGIN HUMOUR RIGHT IS THE THING THAT'S DIFFICULT TO PINPOINT – TOO MANY WERE JUST PUNS ON THE VIRGIN NAME WHICH IS NOTHING NEW. WHILST I WAS AMAZED AT THE AMOUNT OF EFFORT STUDENTS HAD PUT INTO DEVELOPING AND PRESENTING THEIR IDEAS, I WAS DISAPPOINTED AT THE GENERAL LACK OF FRESHNESS OR ORIGINALITY – NOTHING STOPPED ME IN MY TRACKS.
GINNIE LEATHAM

THE SUCCESSFUL ENTRIES STOOD OUT BECAUSE THEY WERE SIMPLE, SURPRISING OR JUST PLAIN FUNNY. A LOT OF STUDENTS SEEMED TO SETTLE FOR WORK THAT WAS SAFE AND FAMILIAR RATHER THAN PUSH FOR SOMETHING CHALLENGING AND DIFFERENT. STRONG TECHNICAL SKILLS WERE DEMONSTRATED BY MANY, BUT IT SEEMED THAT TOO MUCH TIME HAD BEEN SPENT ON THE MACS, TOO LITTLE ON THE IDEAS. **ADAM TUCKER**

Adam Tucker
BMP DDB

Ginnie Leatham
Virgin Atlantic

Mark Reddy
BMP DDB

Second

Student
Sam Lachlan

Tutors
David Beaugeard
Paul Minott

College
Bath Spa University College

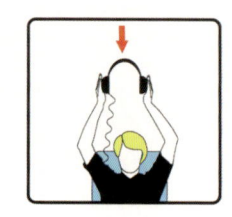

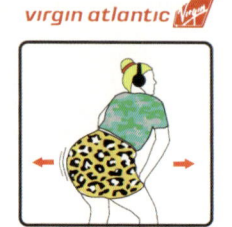

Second

Students
Isabel Octavio De Toledo
Diego Perez
Jose Luis Varon Garces

Tutors
Florencia Montes
Marcelo Montes

College
The School Agency

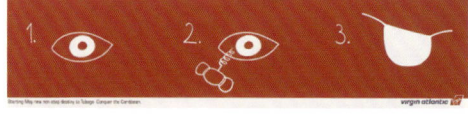

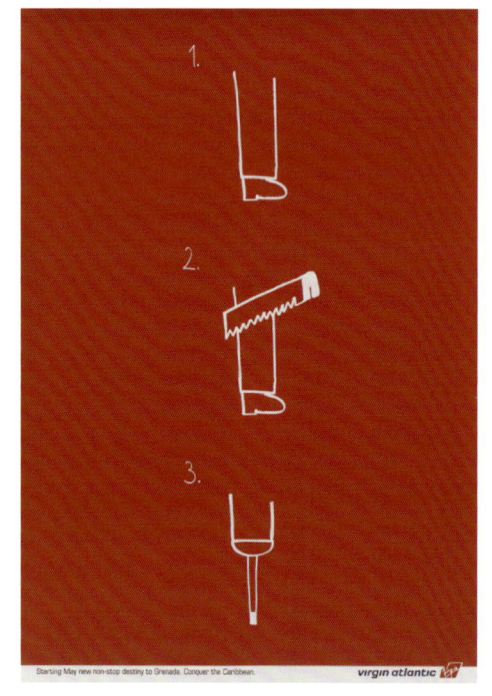

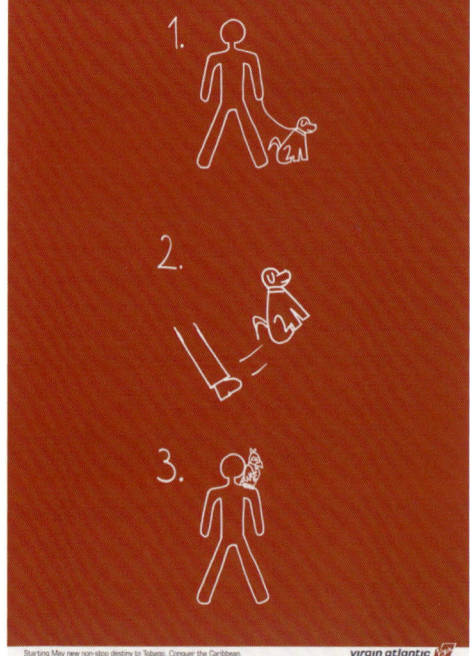

Commendation

Students
Scott Bell
Jennifer Handline

Tutor
Jerry Torchia

College
Miami Ad School

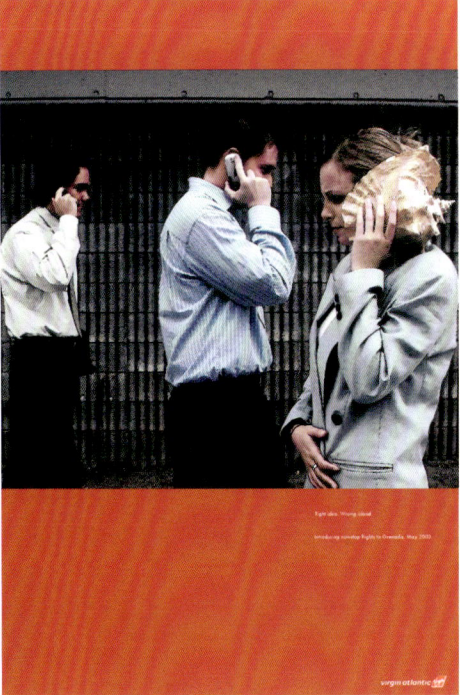

Students
Paul Kinsella
Cynthia Wong

Tutors
Lin Sinclair
Mike Moran
Mark Lamey

College
University of Central Lancashire

Student
Michael Duncan

Tutors
Peter Benson
Greg Rendell

College
Swindon College

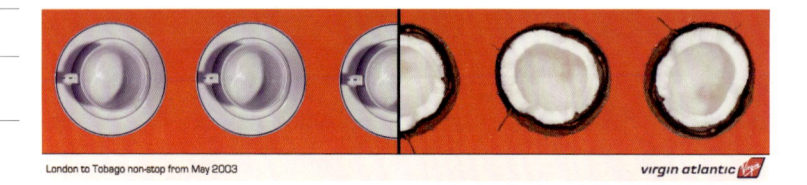

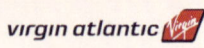

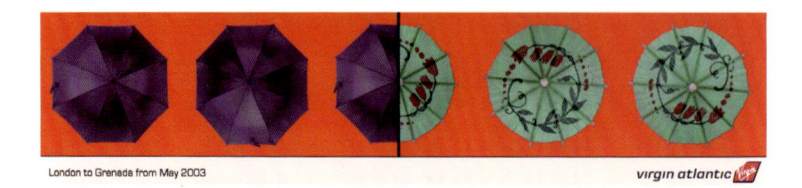

Students
Melissa Bell
Christian Osmers

Tutor
Melinda Mettler

College
Academy of Art College

LONDON · GRENADA

new nonstops. may 2003. virgin atlantic

White Castle

D&AD Student Awards 2003

To whom it may concern

I do not mean to be snobbish, but I am the most beautiful woman in this world. People think I am so lucky to be this beautiful. After all this is the part of the reason the prince kissed me when I was poisoned and saved my life.

But sometimes I feel that if I was not beautiful my life could have been different. My maternal mother died after giving birth to me, I am still not over that. My father remarried soon after and my stepmother was a beautiful but very cold woman. She never showed me affection; in fact she threw me out of the castle. I still remember the time I was nearly shot by an arrow. Sometimes, I get flash backs and scream at night. And that apple! I am not able to look at an apple to this day. I went on to develop an eating disorder because of my fear of eating. My husband loves me, but I have this suspicion he may be a necrophiliac.

I wish I were not this beautiful. If I were not born beautiful, I would have lead normal and quiet life and would not have been this traumatised. Maybe I should consider a plastic surgery. Can you recommend someone good?

Yours Truly

Snow White

SPONSORED BY
TRANSPORT FOR LONDON

Transport for London

RADIO ADVERTISING

THE BRIEF REFLECTING LONDON'S ETHNIC AND CULTURAL DIVERSITY, CREATE A RADIO ADVERT TO PROMOTE THE BENEFITS OF LATE NIGHT PUBLIC TRANSPORT IN THE CAPITAL. DEMONSTRATE THE SAFETY AND EASE WITH WHICH THESE MULTI-MODAL METHODS OF GETTING HOME CAN BE USED, PARTICULARLY TO GROUPS WHO MAY FEEL VULNERABLE USING THE SERVICE AT PRESENT.

JUDGES' COMMENTS PUBLIC TRANSPORT AND SAFETY? THAT'S TOUGH! THE WINNER ANSWERED THE BRIEF WITH ORIGINALITY AND COMPREHENSION. **TED HEATH**

ORIGINAL AND SIMPLE, THE WINNING RADIO AD CAME ACROSS VERY WELL AND GOT STRAIGHT TO THE POINT. **SANDRA FINLAY**

THE WINNER CHALLENGED THE LISTENER BY NOT HAVING THE EXPECTED ANSWERS. **INNES FERGUSON**

Tim Harris
Eardrum

Steve Spence
Scholz & Friends

Sandra Finlay
Transport for London

Ted Heath
M&C Saatchi

Innes Ferguson
Transport for London

Alun Howell
Ogilvy

First

Students
Rob Ferrara
Liz Franklin

Tutors
Leah Klein
Julie Wright
John Merriman

College
Buckinghamshire Chilterns University College

The Knowledge

A wannabe taxi driver is preparing to take his test for The Knowledge.

Examiner Take a seat please. This is the oral part of the examination. You will have to pass this in order to complete The Knowledge.

(pause)

Now, it is 2:30 in the morning. You are asked to pick someone up from Trafalgar Square and take them to Petticoat Lane. What is the quickest route?

Cabbie Well, the quickest, and the cheapest route would be to take the tube to London Bridge and then get the bus from there to Petticoat Lane. There's one that goes there 24 hours a day. (Pause). 'Course those minicabs are licensed now too. That'd be another option.

(sharp intake of breath from examiners)

FVO For further information on late night travel in London, from taxis, to buses, to tubes to trains, visit the Transport for London website at www.tfl.gov.uk, also available 24 hours a day.

Examiner (in a patronising tone) Thank you Mr Blackmore, we'll be in touch.

Second

Students
Ben Middleton
Stuart Outhwaite

Tutors
Zelda Malan
David Morris
Lyndon Mallet

College
Buckinghamshire Chilterns University College

Radio 1 – Tequila to tea

This is the first of five radio ads which feature the sounds of nightlife (pubs, clubs, restaurants) dissolving/resolving into the sounds of home and sleep.

Music Samba and carnival music plays. The rhythm gradually simplifies. Music gradually reduces down and instruments fall away and fade out. A lone cow bell is left chiming, which resolves itself into the chink chink of a teaspoon stirring in a cup.

VO Transport for London now offers services 24 hours a day, taking you home safely from your tequila to your tea.

For more information check out www.tfl.gov.uk

Radio 2 – Dancing to dreaming

This is the second of five 30 second radio ads which feature the sounds of nightlife (pubs, clubs, restaurants etc) dissolving/resolving into the sounds of home and sleep.

Music Pounding dance music plays. The various keyboard chords and samples that make up the tune gradually dissolve and fade out, leaving a single pounding beat, which resolves itself into the rhythmical sounds of someone happily snoring in bed.

VO Transport for London now offers services 24 hours a day, taking you home safely from your dancing to your dreaming.

For more information check out www.tfl.gov.uk

Radio 3 – Culture vultures to early birds

This is the third of five 30 second radio ads which feature the sounds of nightlife (pubs, clubs, restaurants etc) dissolving/resolving into the sounds of home and sleep.

SFX The familiar sounds of a busy restaurant start. Gradually the individual sounds, such as bottles being corked open and knives scratching on plates fade out one by one, until all we can hear is the soft sound of wine glasses being toasted together, which resolves itself into the sounds of small morning birds chirping.

VO Transport for London now offers services 24 hours a day, taking you home safely from the culture vultures to the early birds.

For more information check out www.tfl.gov.uk

Second continued

Students
Ben Middleton
Stuart Outhwaite

Tutors
Zelda Malan
David Morris
Lyndon Mallet

College
Buckinghamshire Chilterns University College

Radio 4 – Moshing to morning

This is the fourth of five 30 second radio ads which feature the sounds of nightlife (pubs, clubs, restaurants etc) dissolving/resolving into the sounds of home and sleep.

Music Highly energetic rock music blares out with crashing cymbals and powerchords, the music builds towards a classic rock climax. High screaming guitar solo begins and as it becomes higher pitched it resolves itself into the beeping of an alarm clock going off.

VO Transport for London now offers services 24 hours a day, taking you home safely from your moshing to your morning.

For more information check out www.tfl.gov.uk

Radio 5 – Breakdancing to breakfast

This is the fifth of five 30 second radio ads which feature the sounds of nightlife (pubs, clubs, restaurants etc) dissolving/resolving into the sounds of home and sleep.

Music The sound of a hip hop record plays with funk samples, a heavy beat and scratching, all of which gradually dissolve and fade out, leaving the sound of a deejay scratching a record which resolves itself into the sound of someone buttering their toast.

VO Transport for London now offers services 24 hours a day, taking you home safely from your breakdancing to your breakfast.

For more information check out www.tfl.gov.uk

Commendation

Students
James Birchall
Christen Brestrup

Tutors
Lin Sinclair
Mike Moran
Mark Lamey

College
University of Central Lancashire

Instructor 1

Instructor (masc. voice) Hello class, in tonight's self-defence lesson I'll be teaching you the technique of safe travel around London at night.

These techniques are designed to provide you with the maximum protection.

Ok class, follow me…

Raise your right arm like this…

SFX Rustling of clothes.

Instructor Are we all ready?

Now shout… 'TAXI!'

VO For more information on safe travel at night, log on to www.tfl.gov.uk. Transport for London. Taking you safely door-to-door.

Students
Vicki Heath
Kelly McDonald

Tutors
Leah Klein
Lyndon Mallet
Julie Wright

College
Buckinghamshire Chilterns University College

Transport For London – Party Pooper

SFX Just finished football match on the T.V. Group of men chatting in the background.

Guy 1 (boring party-pooper) Right, I'm off.

Guy 2 (excitable) Arrh, come on, we haven't even got the Playstation out yet.

Guy 3 (nagging tone) Don't be boring Dave.

Guy 1 I just don't want to get stuck travelling late through London.

Guy 2 You only live four doors away.

SFX Background noises fade.

Guy 1 Taxi!

SFX 1 Taxi door shuts, then rev. of engine.

SFX 2 Bleeps, 'mind the doors' then Tube door shuts.

Guy 1 Single to…

SFX 3 Air breaks blast, then creaky bus door shuts.

SFX 4 Home door shuts, the knocker taps against the door.

Guy 1 I'm home love.

VO Contact Transport for London at www.tfl.gov.uk and you can travel safely anytime, day or night, from door to door to door to door.

Students
Hayley Davis
Lindsay Gill

Tutors
Bobert Bowdery
Frank Holmes
Greg Mills

College
University of Gloucestershire

Surprise!

Female voice 1 (standard recorded answerphone voice) You have four new messages.

SFX Beep

SFX Noise of Underground station platform in the background

Male voice 1 (East End 'Jack the Lad' voice) Johnny boy! Heard your wife's outta town. On the tube to your parrtay!!

Wicked!

SFX Beep

FV2 and 3 (American voice – with English voice adding her name within this message – in sexy, sultry tones) Hi! It's Roxie – and Trish – from the Starlight Club. We're in a cab to your place to do our thang after midnight.

SFX Beep

SFX Faint clubbing music can be heard in the background

MV2 (Afro-Caribbean voice, almost shouting) Mate! Gettin' the bus to yours with the guys from the squad… Wooo!

SFX Beep

SFX Taxi noise in the background

(bright, breezy voice of wife) Hi darling. Surprise! I'll be home tonight after all. I'm in a taxi from the station. See you in a sec if you're still awake. Love you!

MVO (well-spoken English accent, with a soft tone) Transport for London. Here when you need us… AND when you don't! www.tfl.gov.uk

Students
Imran Patel
Dave Prater

Tutors
Leah Klein
Julie Wright

College
Buckinghamshire Chilterns University College

Deliveryman

(in style of a Fed Ex ad)

SFX Sound of urban traffic, i.e. Buses, cars, motorcycles, whooshes, horns etc.

MVO (enthusiastic American accent) Hi, I'm someone you can rely on because I work for a delivery service like no other. We're in action 24/7, which means we're always available for those important over-night deliveries. I'm part of this super integrated distribution service, which uses road and rail to guarantee speed and efficiency. We transport safely, promptly and straight to your door. I'm part of a special team you can always depend on. Who am I?

SFX Bus bell dings.

MVO (back to his original cockney accent). Hold tight darling. (beeps). I'm a bus driver with Transport For London, and I deliver you.

If you want to know more about our 24-hour express deliveries visit www.tfl.gov.uk

MVO (puts on American accent again). Transport For London, when you absolutely, positively need over-night delivering.

From: Richard Newell & Pete Williams
- 3rd Yr (BA) Advertising
- University of Gloucestershire

- How far would you go?
    We'd keep going until our pen runs out.

Until our pen runs out, until our pen runs out,

Until our pen runs out, until our pen runs out, until our pen runs out, until our pen runs out, until our pen runs out, until our pen runs out, until our pen runs out, until our pen runs out, until our pen runs out, until our pen runs out, until our pen runs out, until our pen runs out, until our pen runs out, **UNTIL OUR PEN RUNS OUT,** until our pen runs out, **UNTIL OUR PEN RUNS OUT,** until our pen runs out, until our pen runs out, until our pen runs out, until our pen runs out, until our pen runs out, until our pen runs out, until our pen runs out, until our pen runs out, until our pen runs out, until our pen runs out, until our pen runs out, until our pen runs out, until our pen runs out, **UNTIL OUR PEN RUNS OUT,** until our pen runs out, until our pen runs out until our pen runs out, **Until our pen runs out.**

Until our pen runs out, until our pen runs out, until our pen runs out, until our pen runs out, until our pen runs out, **UNTIL OUR PEN RUNS OUT,** until our pen runs out, until our pen runs out, until our pen runs out, until our pen runs out, **UNTIL OUR PEN RUNS OUT,** until our pen runs out, until our pen runs out, until our pen runs out, until our pen runs out, until our pen runs out, until our pen runs out, until our pen runs out, until our pen runs out, until our pen runs out, until our pen runs out, until our pen runs out, until our pen runs out, until our pen runs out, until our pen runs out, (until our pen runs out) until our pen runs for its life, until our pen runs out, until our pen runs out, until our pen runs out, until our pen runs out, until our pen runs out, until our pen runs out.

- Until our pen runs out, until our pen runs out, until our pen runs out, until our pen runs out, until our pen runs out, until our pen runs out, until our pen runs, until our pen runs out, until our pen runs out!!, until our pen runs out, until it runs out! until our pen runs out, until our pen runs out, until our pen runs out, **UNTIL OUR PEN RUNS OUT!!!!** until our pen runs out! until our pen runs out, until our pen runs out, until our **PEN RUNS OUT!** until our pen runs out, until our pen runs out until our pen runs out, until our pen runs out, until our pen runs out, until our pen runs out, until our pen runs out, until **OUR PEN RUNS OUT!** until our pen runs out, until our pen runs out, until our pen runs out, until our pen runs out, until our pen runs out, until our pen runs out.

- WHAT DO YOU REALLY WANT?

- WE REALLY WANT OUR PEN TO RUN OUT

Until our pen runs out, until our pen runs out, until our pen runs out, until our pen runs out, until our pen runs out, until our pen runs out, until our pen runs out, until our pen runs out!!!!
Until our pen runs out
Until our pen runs out
until our pen runs out, until our pen runs out.

UNTIL OUR PEN RUNS OUT

Until our pen runs out
until our pen runs out, until our pen runs out, until our pen runs out, until our pen runs out, until our pen runs out, until our pen runs out, until our pen runs out, **until our pen runs out,** until our pen runs out, until our pen runs out, until our pen runs out
en p   until ou
 runs ou   n   u
p ns out, until our pen p

SPONSORED BY
TISCALI

TISCALI

STREAMING

THE BRIEF CREATE A 30 TO 60 SECOND MOVIE STREAM TO BE USED ON-LINE TO INTRODUCE A VIEWING FACILITY ENABLING CUSTOMERS TO SEE DESIRABLE HOLIDAY DESTINATIONS. BE SENSITIVE TO A TARGET AUDIENCE OF OVER 55'S WHO ARE CULTURED, COMFORTABLY OFF AND READY TO DO ALL THOSE THINGS THEY'VE ALWAYS MEANT TO. ILLUSTRATE THE IMMEDIACY OF THE TECHNOLOGY IN SHOWING WHICH PLACES THEY COULD 'GET AWAY FROM IT ALL'.

JUDGES' COMMENTS IT WAS ENCOURAGING TO SEE THAT THE MAJORITY OF ENTRANTS HAD PLACED IDEAS ABOVE EXECUTION. THAT SAID, THE STANDARD OF PRESENTATION WAS MIND BLOWING AND IT PROVES TO ME THAT STREAMING, AS A MEDIA CHANNEL, HAD OPENED UP FRESH MINDS TO THE CREATIVE USE OF ANIMATION. **STEVE DIXON**

SEVERAL STRONG ENTRIES DELIVERED POWERFUL AND ORIGINAL ANIMATIONS IN RESPONSE TO THE BRIEF. ALL THE ENTRIES WERE COMPETENT, SEVERAL OUTSTANDING – OVERALL A VERY IMPRESSIVE SET OF WORK. **MARK HARRIS**

THE WINNING ENTRY HAD HUMOUR AND A CONCEPT THAT WORKED AT DIFFERENT LEVELS, SHOWING THAT THOMAS COOK AND OLDER CUSTOMERS HAVE A SENSE OF FUN IN LINE WITH EXISTING BRAND VALUES. AN EXCELLENT STANDARD OVERALL, WITH SOME STRONG, STIMULATING EXECUTIONS. **KATHARINE BEGG**

Daljit Singh
Digit Digital Experiences

Mark Harris
Tiscali

Katharine Begg
Thomas Cook

Steve Dixon
Propaganda

First

Students
Jonathan Goodall
Rosie Neave

Tutors
Michael Smith
Christian Lloyd

College
Leeds College
of Art and Design

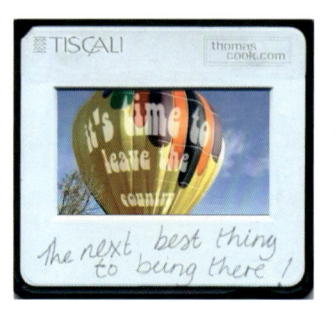

148

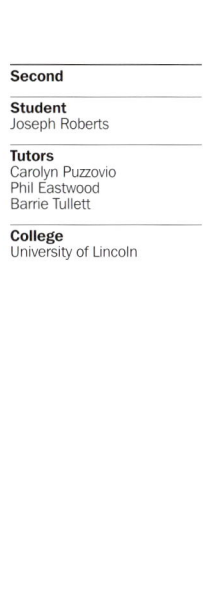

Second

Student
Joseph Roberts

Tutors
Carolyn Puzzovio
Phil Eastwood
Barrie Tullett

College
University of Lincoln

Commendation

Student
Leon Bonaventura

Tutors
Robert De Niet
Calum Mackenzie
Andrea Taylor

College
Surrey Institute of Art and Design University College at Epsom

Student
Nicole Chamberlain

Tutors
Carolyn Puzzovio
Phil Eastwood
Barrie Tullett

College
University of Lincoln

Students
Vanessa Gorman
Hew Fuen Ma

Tutors
Michael Smith
Christian Lloyd

College
Leeds College
of Art and Design

Student
Ray Dauncey

Tutors
David Gardener
Kate Bonella
Paul Smith
Vicky Isley

College
Southampton Institute

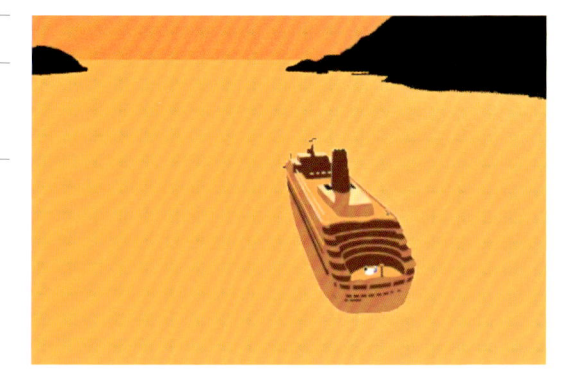

Students
Chris Evans
Craig Hunter

Tutors
Bruce Ingman
Paul Plowman

College
Buckinghamshire Chilterns
University College

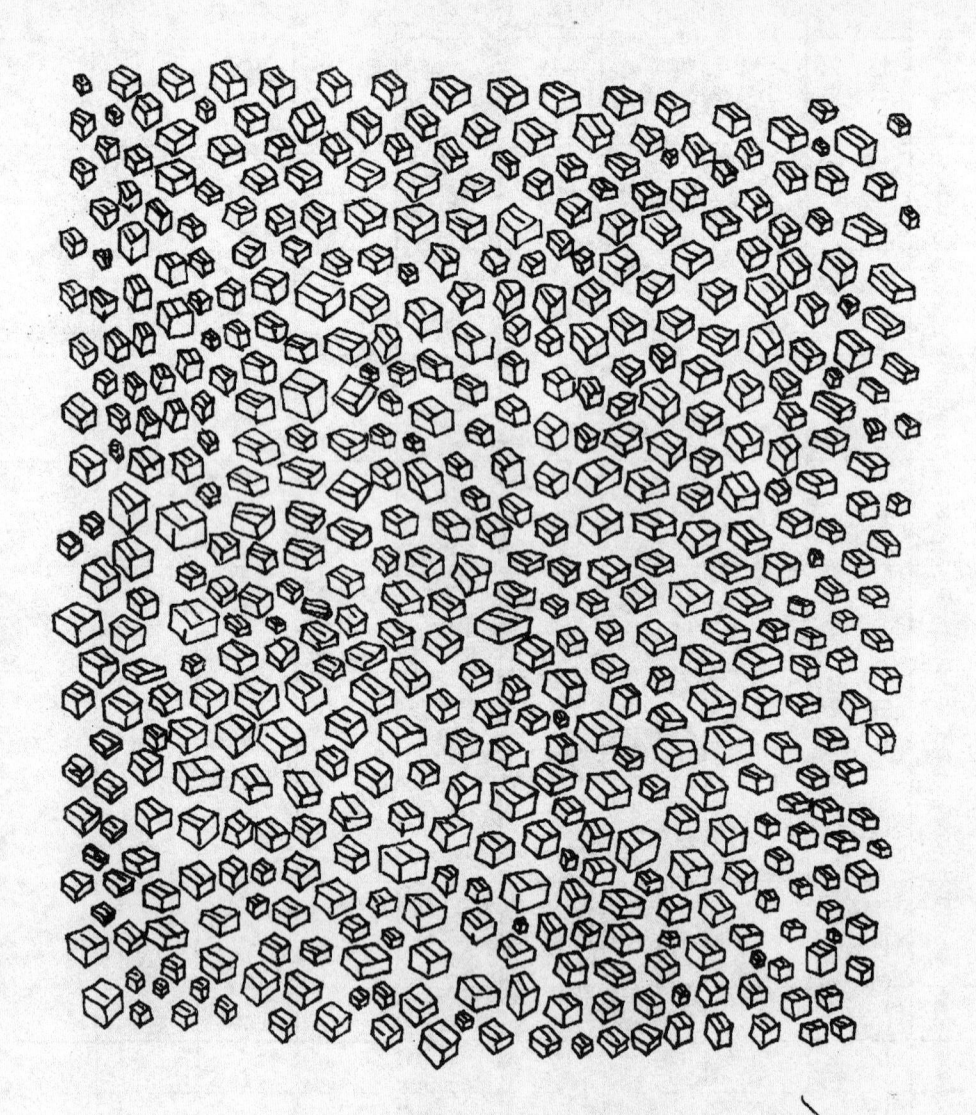

(There is a ferret in one of these boxes.)
by michael simpson age 7¼ From Surrey institute of art and Design!!!

SPONSORED BY AQUENT

AQUENT

TV GRAPHICS

THE BRIEF TELEVISION VIEWERS NOW HAVE THE OPPORTUNITY TO CREATE PERSONALISED SCHEDULES SPECIFIC TO THEIR VIEWING TASTES. DEVELOP A FIVE TO TEN SECOND ON SCREEN IDENTITY SEQUENCE TO BRAND THE PARENT COMPANY, AND DESIGN A SUB-BRAND CHANNEL TAILORED TO A SPECIFIC AGE OR LIFESTYLE GROUP.

JUDGES' COMMENTS I WAS HOPING FOR SOME 'OUT OF THE BOX' THINKING, AND THE CREATIVE APPROACH OF THE WINNER WAS OUTSTANDING. THE VERY ESSENCE OF PERSONALISED TV HAD BEEN SUCCESSFULLY ENCAPSULATED. IT WAS AN IDEAL SOLUTION, VERY WELL EXECUTED. **MIKE HURST**

THE OVERALL STANDARD WAS GREAT. TECHNICAL AND CREATIVE ABILITY COUPLED WITH GOOD IDEAS, WIT AND KNOWLEDGE OF THE TARGET AUDIENCE. THE WINNER REALLY PUSHED THE BOUNDARY OF WHAT INTERACTIVE TV COULD BE… ONE OF FEW WHO WENT BEYOND WHAT IS CURRENTLY ON OFFER, AND BROUGHT NEW AND INTERESTING IDEAS TO THE BRIEF. A STRONG RESPONSE WHICH MADE ME WANT TO START WATCHING THAT CHANNEL. **KIMBERLY KAPNER**

THE WINNER WAS A BOLD, ORIGINAL AND BALLSY SOLUTION THAT NOT ONLY ANSWERED THE BRIEF, BUT WAS CONCEPTUALLY ON MUCH HIGHER GROUND THAN THE REST OF THE ENTRIES – AND ALSO MUCH CURRENT TV BRANDING. **ELLIOT CHAFFER**

Marcus Jones
Lambie-Nairn

Kimberly Kapner
Aquent

Andy Stewart
Aquent

Mike Hurst
BSkyB

Elliot Chaffer
Milk Communications

First

Student
Tim Smyllie

Tutor
Geoffrey Thomas-Shaw

College
Chelsea College
of Art and Design

154

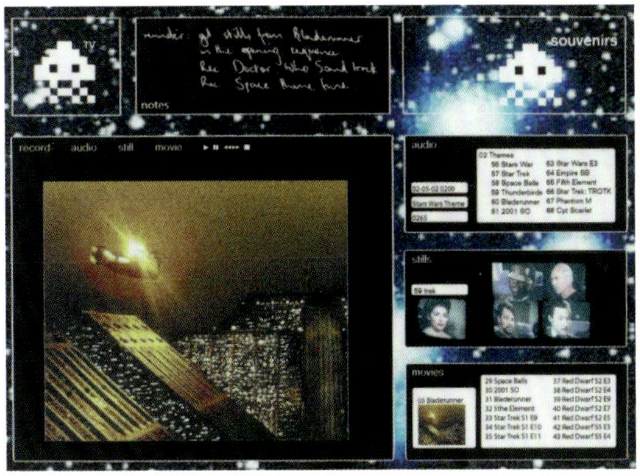
tv
notes
souvenirs
record audio still movie
audio
stills
movies

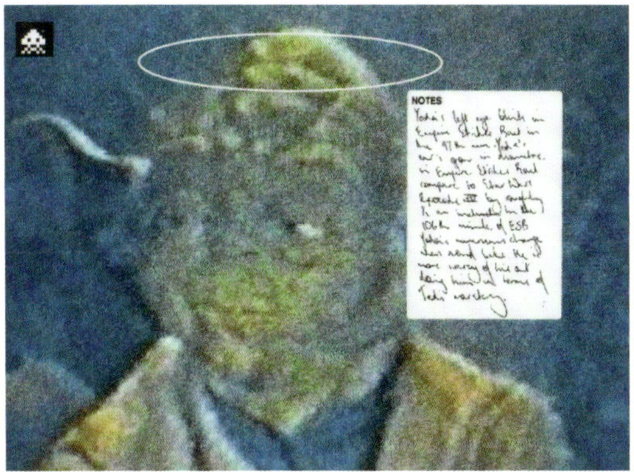
NOTES

EXTERMINATE
flick
What else is on?
Thunderbirds S4 E5
Thunderbirds S3 E2
Thunderbirds S10 E7
Thunderbirds S7 E5
Thunderbirds S4 E8
Star Trek S6 E9
Star Trek S6 E6
Star Trek S6 E3
Star Trek S20 E7
Star Trek S12 E6

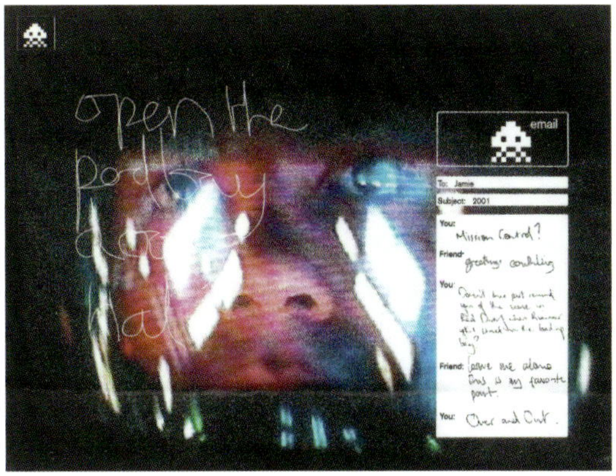
email
To: Jamie
Subject: 2001
You:
Friend:
You:
Friend:
You:

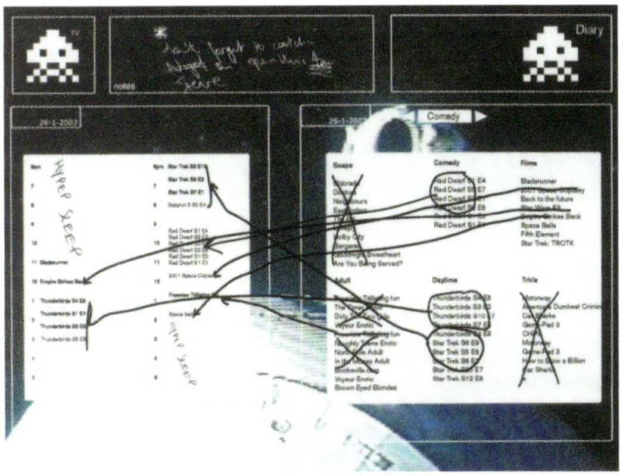
tv
notes
Diary
Comedy

REMINDER 1420 15-02-03
MAY THE FORCE BE WITH YOU

Second

Student
Christopher Butler

Tutors
David Gill
Andy Holt
Alan Summers

College
North Wales School
of Art and Design

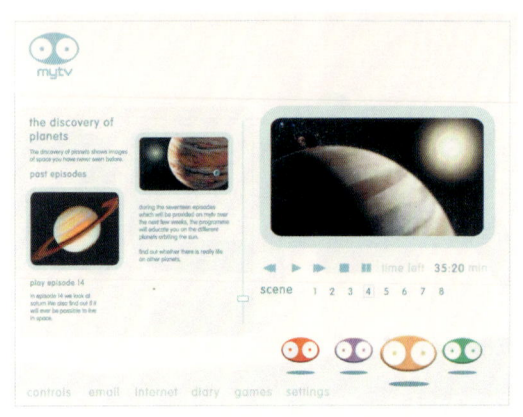

By selecting the programme [brought to foreground] the viewer can access supporting information.

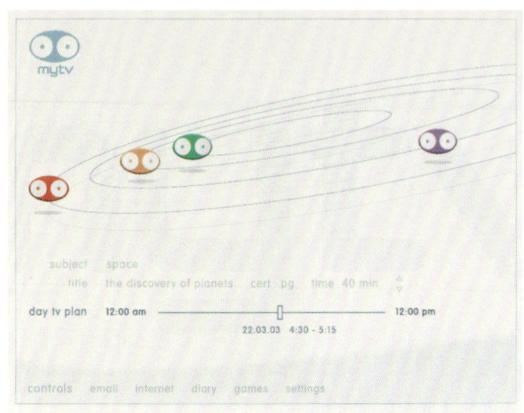

Once a particular programme has been selected, the time of showing can be ascertained by use of the time line.

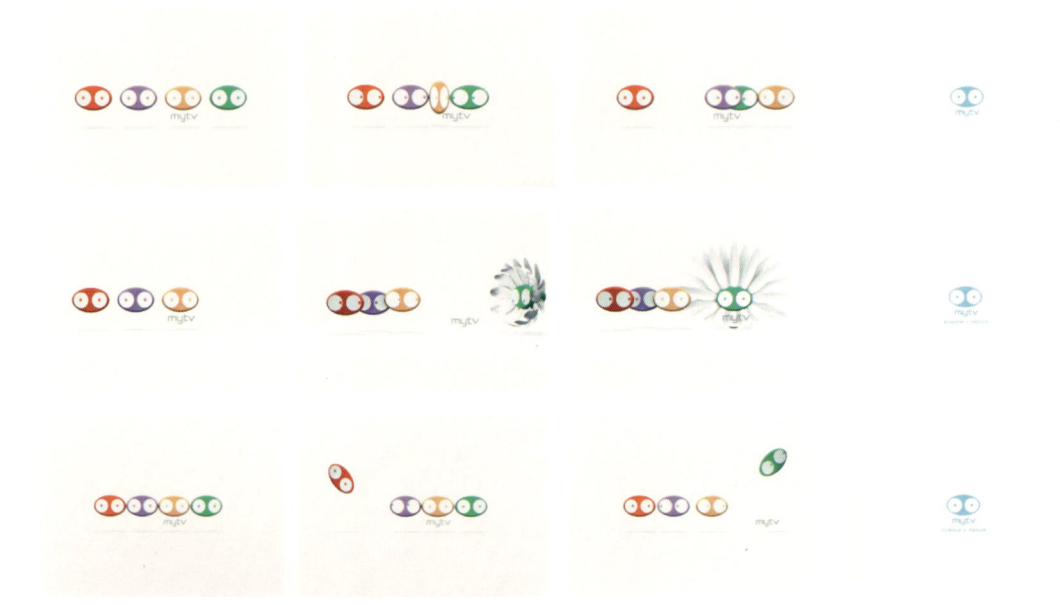

Optional control panel displayed during the viewing of programme.

156

Commendation

Student
Stephen Flynn

Tutors
David Herbert
Gordon Robertson

College
Duncan of Jordanstone
College of Art

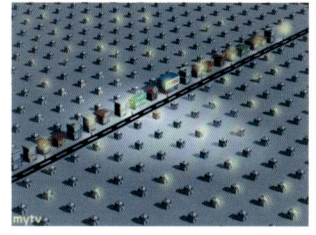

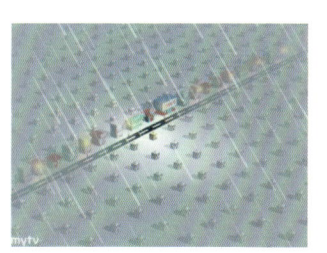

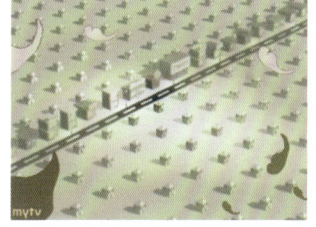

Commendation

Student
Simon Ramsay

Tutors
David Herbert
Gordon Robertson

College
Duncan of Jordanstone
College of Art

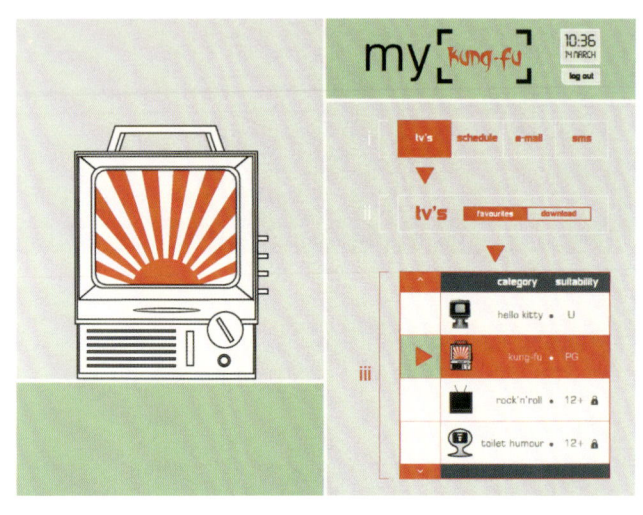

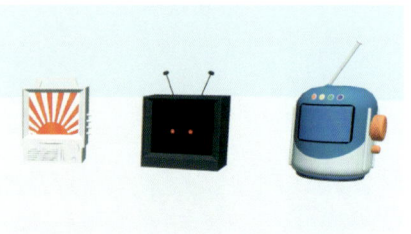

Students
Chris Baxter
Lawrence Mann

Tutor
Graham Tansley

College
Leeds College
of Art and Design

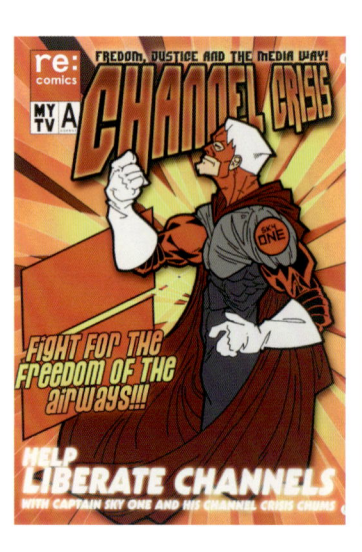

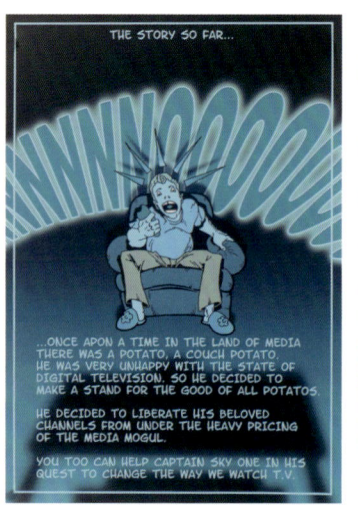

Student
Edward Whatton

Tutors
Peter Benson
Greg Rendell

College
Swindon College

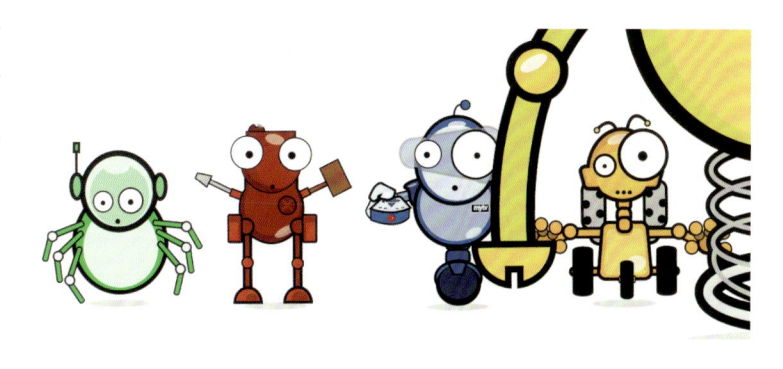

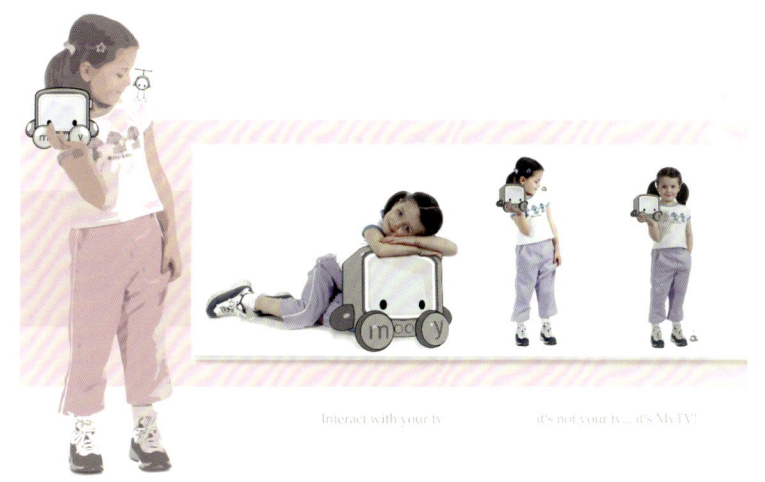

Student
James Roadley-Battin

Tutor
Chris Hinton

College
De Montfort University

159

ECA. "WHAT DO YOU REALLY WANT?", Paiva Bruhn.

WORLD PEACE

ECA. "What do you really want!", Paiva Bruhn.

SAVE THE DOLPHINS

ECA. "Where are we going?", Paiva Bruhn.

WHERE ARE WE GOING?

SPONSORED BY
MTV

TV SHORT

THE BRIEF PRODUCE A THOUGHT PROVOKING SHORT-FILM DRAMATISING ISSUES OF TOLERANCE TO APPEAL TO BRITAIN'S 'DISENFRANCHISED' YOUTH. ITS TONE SHOULD ATTEMPT TO CAPTURE AND EMPOWER YOUNG PEOPLE WITHOUT ALIENATING OR PATRONISING THEM.

JUDGES' COMMENTS WE WERE LOOKING FOR AN ARRESTING, EMOTIVE DRAMATISATION OF THE ISSUE OF TOLERANCE. THE CHALLENGE WAS TO MAKE THE COMMUNICATION POWERFUL AND COMPLETE, WITHOUT RESORTING TO CLICHÉ. THERE WAS SOME INTERESTING CRAFT AND FILMIC ENTERPRISE ON DISPLAY, BUT NOTHING STARTLINGLY ORIGINAL OR EXCITING. DISAPPOINTINGLY, NO ONE FILM ADDRESSED THE BRIEF IN A COMPELLING WAY, AND THERE WAS A GENERAL LACK OF REAL UNDERSTANDING INTO THE PRINCIPLES OF COMMUNICATION. TOO MANY FILMS WERE EITHER A LITTLE CRASS IN THEIR SIMPLICITY OR INCONCLUSIVE IN THEIR STORY-TELLING. ON THIS BASIS, AND WITH MUCH RELUCTANCE, THE JUDGES FELT NO WORK WAS WORTHY OF BEING SELECTED. **JAMES SCROGGS**

MOST OF THE ENTRIES FOCUSED ON LOOKING GREAT AND USING FANCY CUTS RATHER THAN DELIVERING A GREAT SCRIPT WITH A STRONG IDEA. **CECILIA DUFILS**

ENTRIES GENERALLY SHOWED A TENDENCY TO SETTLE FOR PAROCHIAL IDEAS RATHER THAN EXPLORING ORIGINAL OR STRIKING IDEAS. THERE WERE POCKETS OF LIGHT, BUT NONE THAT WE FELT REALLY DESERVED A PLACE IN THIS PRESTIGIOUS ANNUAL. **JORDAN MCGARRY**

Cecilia Dufils
Mother

James Scroggs
MTV

Jordan McGarry
Shots

Georgia Cooke
MTV

HOW FAR WOULD YOU GO?

AN**UAL**

CALL FOR ENTRIES

SPONSORED BY
AGFA MONOTYPE

AGFA | Monotype

TYPOGRAPHY

THE BRIEF DESIGN A SERIES OF A5 SUBSCRIPTION MAILERS FOR CREATIVE REVIEW. ATTEMPT TO ENCAPSULATE THE ORIGINALITY AND IMAGINATIVE FREEDOM THE REVIEW PROMOTES VIA THE USE OF EXPRESSIVE AND ILLUSTRATIVE LETTERFORMS. ALL APPROACHES ARE VALID FROM KITSCH TO COOL, HUMOROUS TO SERIOUS AND BEYOND.

JUDGES' COMMENTS THE BRIEF WAS A REAL GIFT FOR ANYONE INTERESTED IN EXPLORING THE EXPRESSIVE POTENTIAL OF LETTERFORMS. I WAS LOOKING FOR A WINNER THAT I CONSIDERED TO BE BEAUTIFUL. BEAUTY FOR ME, IN THIS INSTANCE, BEING AN IMAGINATIVE AND ORIGINAL SOLUTION THAT NOT ONLY ANSWERED THE BRIEF, BUT THAT STOOD OUT FROM THE REST AESTHETICALLY. **SEBASTIAN LESTER**

A LOT OF ENTRIES WERE ONE SIDED – EITHER CONCENTRATING MAINLY ON EXPERIMENTATION OR MAINLY ON CREATIVE REVIEW. HOWEVER, THE OVERALL QUALITY AND DIVERSITY OF THE FINAL SELECTION OF WORK MADE IT TOO DIFFICULT TO SELECT A CLEAR WINNER. **NATHAN GALE**

THERE WERE SO MANY CONTRASTING ARGUMENTS ABOUT ALL THE WORK THAT WAS FINALLY SELECTED THAT IT FELT FAIRER NOT TO GIVE ONE PIECE OF WORK THE FIRST PRIZE. THE OVERALL STANDARD WAS MIXED. TYPOGRAPHY NEEDS TO BE HANDLED WITH CARE AND SENSITIVITY – IF THE FINISHED PIECE LOOKS MESSY, THEN THE TYPEFACE USED PROBABLY COULDN'T DO THE JOB… STUDENTS WERE TRYING TOO HARD. **DOMENIC LIPPA**

Alan Kitching
The Typography Workshop

Sebastian Lester
AGFA Monotype

Julie Strawson
AGFA Monotype

Domenic Lippa
Lippa Pearce

Nathan Gale
Creative Review

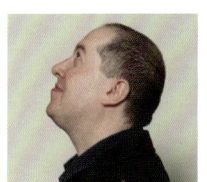

Second

Student
Pie Lee-Mun

Tutors
Kelvin Bulton
Bal Nandra

College
Birmingham Institute
of Art and Design

164

Second

Student
Anna Hjertqvist

Tutor
Marc Wood

College
Central Saint Martins/
College of Art and Design

Commendation

Student
Iain Hector

Tutor
Paul Shakespeare

College
Southampton Institute

Student
Danny Perrett

Tutors
Malcolm Jobling
Nick Jeeves

College
Dunstable College

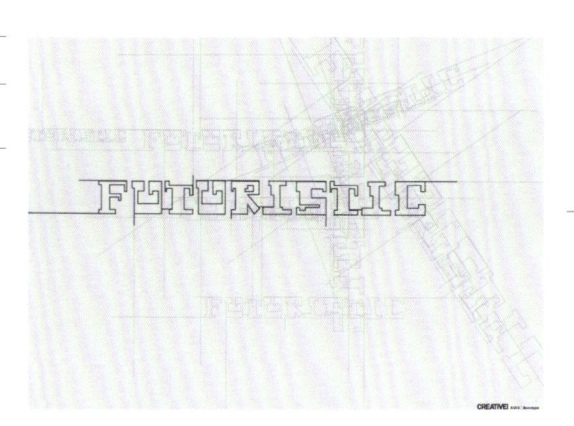

Student
David Peasland

Tutor
Zoë Patterson

College
Edinburgh College of Art

Student
Georgina Hewitt

Tutor
Nigel Robinson

College
Buckinghamshire Chilterns University College

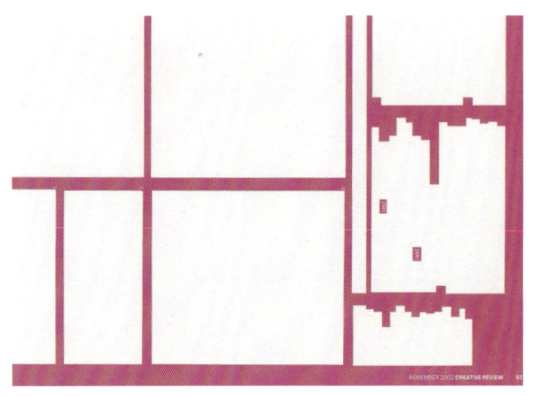

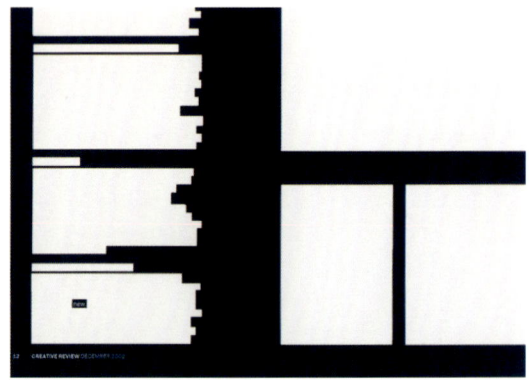

Students
Richard Bell
Jon Eley

Tutors
Lilian Lindblom-Smith
Andrew Grossett

College
Middlesex University

Student
Andrew Bellamy

Tutor
Roger Gould

College
The Arts Institute
Bournemouth

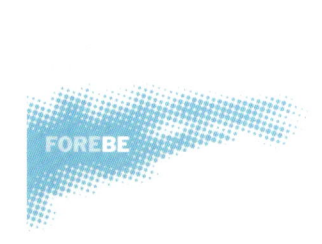

Student
Byron Parr

Tutors
Catherine Dixon
Phil Baines

College
Central Saint Martins/
College of Art and Design

Student
Ryan Joiner

Tutor
Zoë Patterson

College
Edinburgh College of Art

Student
Joshua Leigh

Tutor
Marc Wood

College
Central Saint Martins/
College of Art and Design

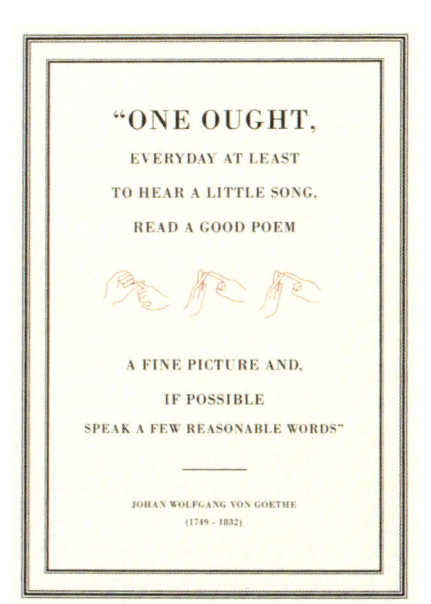

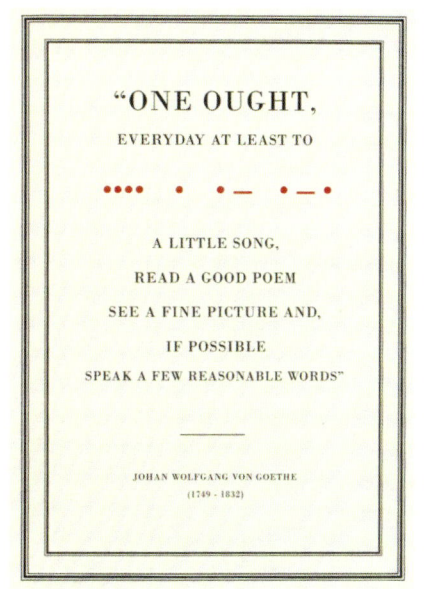

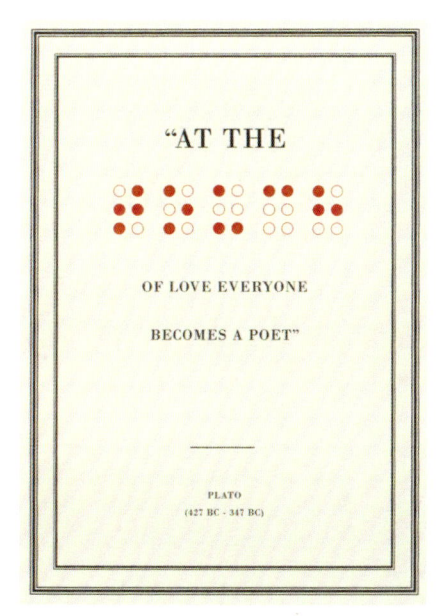

"ONE OUGHT,
EVERYDAY AT LEAST
TO HEAR A LITTLE SONG,
READ A GOOD POEM

A FINE PICTURE AND,
IF POSSIBLE
SPEAK A FEW REASONABLE WORDS"

JOHAN WOLFGANG VON GOETHE
(1749 - 1832)

"ONE OUGHT,
EVERYDAY AT LEAST TO

A LITTLE SONG,
READ A GOOD POEM
SEE A FINE PICTURE AND,
IF POSSIBLE
SPEAK A FEW REASONABLE WORDS"

JOHAN WOLFGANG VON GOETHE
(1749 - 1832)

"AT THE

OF LOVE EVERYONE
BECOMES A POET"

PLATO
(427 BC - 347 BC)

169

02/02/2003 22:33 DAGSAVISEN ANNONSEMOTTAK 0442074079075 AV 740 P001

Ask Jeeves

[What do I really want?]

WEB RESULTS | NEWS RESULTS | SHOPPING RESULTS | Help | Editorial Guidelines

You may find my search results helpful:

Learn Spanish in Ecuador - at Galapagos Spanish School, Ecuador The
If you're serious about learning Spanish, Galapagos Spanish School is your best choice. We provide a variety of language programs, homestays, and a...
From: http://www.galapagos.edu.ec/index.htm

Learn Spanish in Ecuador - at Galapagos Spanish School, Ecuador The
If you're serious about learning Spanish, Galapagos Spanish School is your best choice. We provide a variety of language programs, homestays, and a...
From: http://www.galapagos.edu.ec/englescu.html

AOL Watch
Site seeking and publishing current or former AOL client's complaints.
From: http://www.aolsucks.org/

Comments for General Chemistry Online: FAQ: Atoms, elements, and
Comments ... on General Chemistry Online: FAQ: Atoms, elements, and ions: How do I know that atoms really exist? (made possible by Loquacious)
From: http://greenspun.com/com/generalchemistryonline/atoms/faq/are-atoms-real.sh...

Direct Instruction: The Most Successful Teaching Model
What the Data Really Show: Direct Instruction Really Works!
From: http://www.jefflindsay.com/EducData.shtml

Toda la discografia del artista : Really Gonna Rock Tonight
HOME .. Buscar. DISCOGRAFIA DE : Really Gonna Rock Tonight ... 1 - 1 / 1 ... Resultado : Really Gonna Rock Tonight ... Really Gonna Rock Tonight...
From: http://www.abanicomusical.com/artist/Really+Gonna+Rock+Tonight/0

Anarchism and Other Essays: Anarchism: What It Really Stands For
ANARCHISM: WHAT IT REALLY STANDS FOR. ANARCHY. Ever reviled, accursed, ne'er understood, Thou art the grisly terror of our age.
From: http://sunsite.berkeley.edu/Goldman/Writings/Anarchism/anarchism.html

Toda la discografia del artista : Really Live Worship
Resultado : Really Live Worship ... Really Live Worship ... Glory Of The Lord ... 1 * CD. Really Live Worship ... War Live ... fecha salida:
From: http://www.abanicomusical.com/artist/Really+Live+Worship/0

Really Big Coloring Books - Retail Order Page
Really Big Coloring Books are 32+ pages at 17...
From: http://www.bigcoloringbooks.com/ordretail.htm

Really Big Coloring Books - Order Now
Dinosaurs has 32 exciting pages of Dino coloring, such as Velociraptor, Tyrannosaurus, Seismosaurus, Pretty Jaw and much more. This book includes two...
From: http://www.bigcoloringbooks.com/order.htm

More search results >>

Try these search terms to see more answers:
- My Kinda Place
- Four Spiritual Laws
- Is Jesus God's Son
- Emoticon
- Jesus Savior
- Customer Acquisition Cost
- Smileys Email Emoticons
- Online Sales Statistics
- Grok
- Neurons In Human Brain

YOU MAY FIND THESE OPTIONS USEFUL

Browse by Subject:

Auto	Games	Real Estate	Science
Arts & Entertainment	Health	Recreation	Society
Business	Home & Family	Reference	Sports
Computers	News	Regional	Travel
			World

Additional Links:
Search the Yellow Pages for What do I really want? sponsored by SMARTpages.com

[What do I really want?] Ask

Editorial Guidelines | Submit Your Site | Privacy Statement | Legal Notices
© 2003 Ask Jeeves, Inc.

http://www.ask.com/main/askjeeves.asp?ask=What+do+I+really+want%3&o=0&x=16&y=8

TRUDE HANSEN
BUSKERUD UNIVERSITY COLLEGE
NORWAY

SPONSORED BY
O2

WEBSITE DESIGN

THE BRIEF CREATE A WEBSITE OR MICROSITE THAT EMPHASISES THE BENEFITS OF 'TEXTING' TO THE OVER 40'S. THE SITE SHOULD ENCOURAGE AND INFORM THOSE WHO HAVE NEVER USED THIS SPONTANEOUS AND UNOBTRUSIVE MESSAGING MEDIUM TO 'GET TEXTING', AND ENABLE THE CLIENT TO TRACK CONSUMER RESPONSE WHILE REMAINING TRUE TO THE BOLDNESS AND CLARITY THAT ENCAPSULATES THE BRAND.

JUDGES' COMMENTS THE WINNER WAS THE ONLY ONE WHO THOUGHT BEYOND A STANDARD SOLUTION. HE FOCUSED MORE ON THE IDEA AND COMMUNICATION RATHER THAN THE TECHNOLOGY. **JUSTIN BUCKWELL**

IF YOU'RE A THRUSTING DESIGN STUDENT, THEN UNDERSTANDING THE NEEDS OF A 40-YEAR-OLD NON-TEXT USER MUST BE FORMIDABLE… THE WINNER WAS THE ONLY ENTRANT TO CREATE A SITE THAT WOULD APPEAL TO THE TARGET AUDIENCE WITH A STRONG CREATIVE IDEA, CLEAR SIMPLE INSTRUCTION AND PROFESSIONAL WEB DESIGN STANDARDS. THE WORK WHICH STOOD OUT HAD STRONG TECHNICAL SKILLS BUT – MORE IMPORTANTLY – AN IMAGINATIVE IDEA AT THEIR CORE. IF THE IDEA DOESN'T ENGAGE, THEN NO AMOUNT OF PROFICIENT DESIGN, NAVIGATION OR BRANDING EVER WILL. **WILL HARRIS**

Will Harris
O2

Justin Pearse
New Media Age

Justin Buckwell
@WWW

Alex Harris
VCCP

Alex Maclean
Airside

First

Student
David Leisinger Zhirong

Tutor
Irwanta Salim

College
Temasek Polytechnic

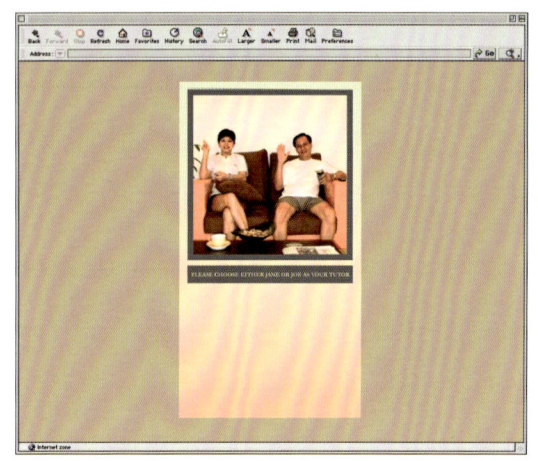

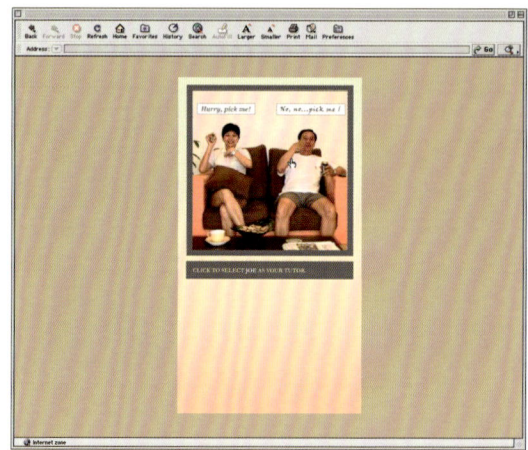

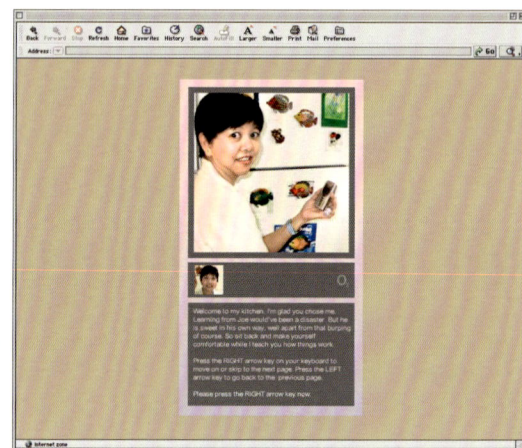

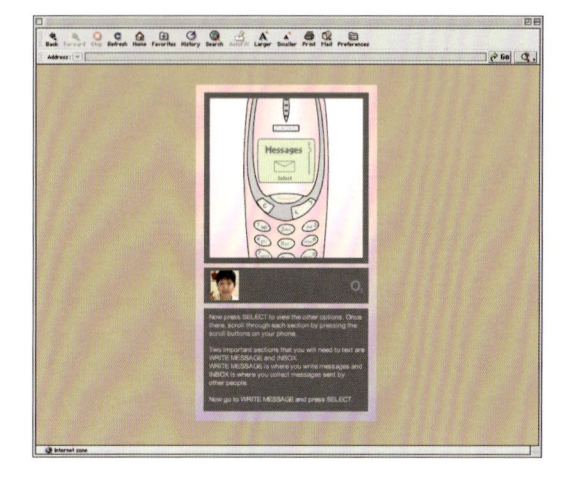

Second

Student
Tom Smith

Tutors
Barry Wenden
Ian Newsham
Paul Wilson

College
University College
Northampton

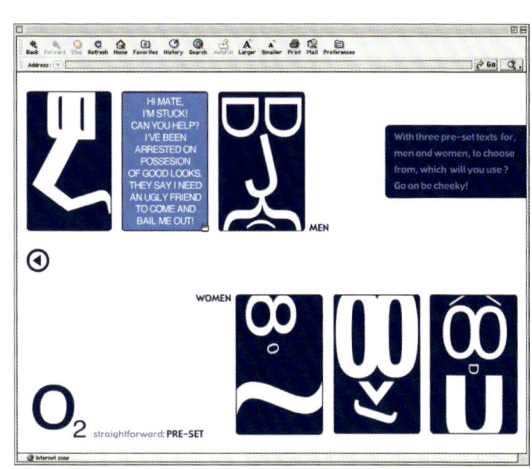

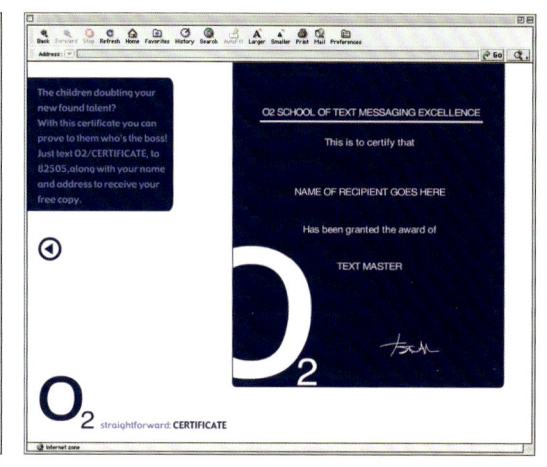

Student
Jason Williams

Tutors
Carolyn Puzzovio
Phil Eastwood
Barrie Tullett

College
University of Lincoln

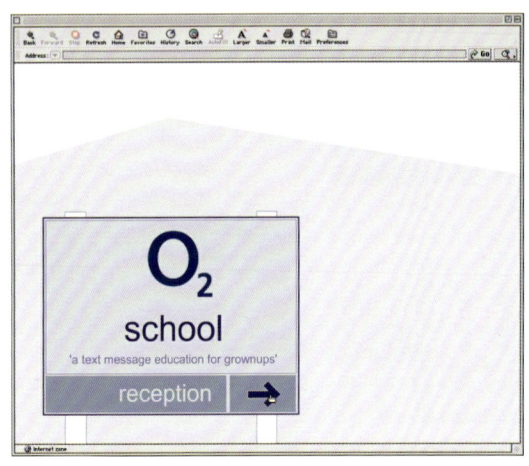

Student
Justin Elliot

Tutors
Mike Davidson
Mario Minichiello
Anne Colwell

College
Loughborough University

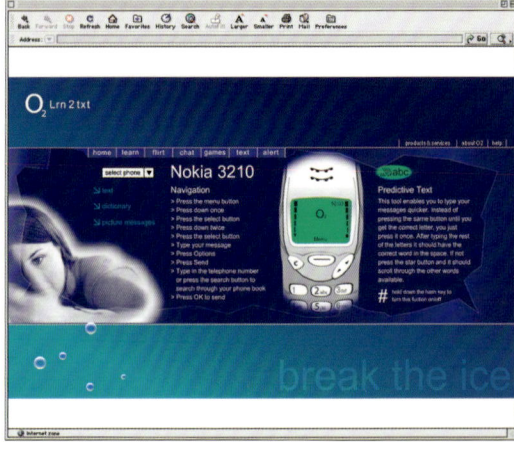

Student
Sam Evans

Tutors
David Gardener
Kate Bonella
Paul Smith
Vicky Isley

College
Southampton Institute

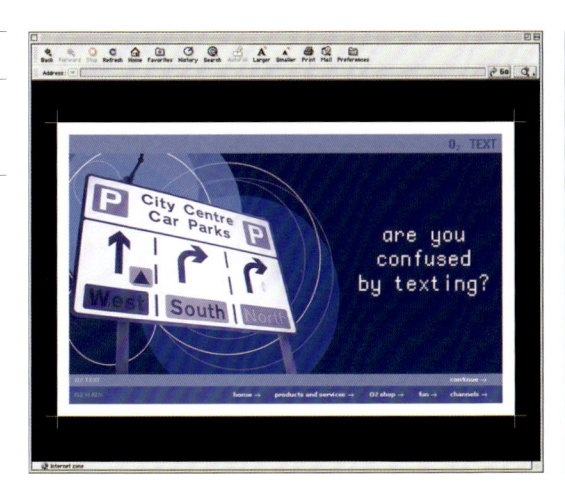

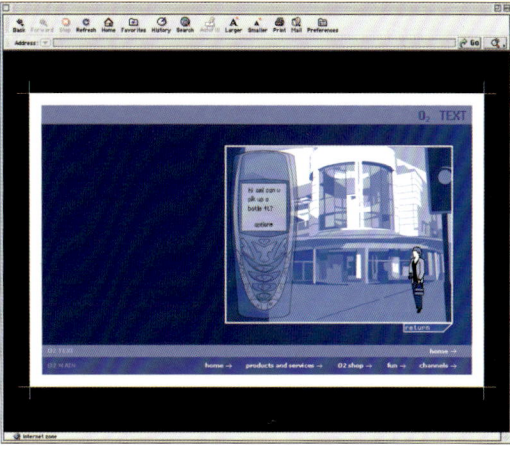

From: LEEDS COLLEGE OF ART AND DESIGN   T: 0532 341244   P02

I really want my Grandy to be lying when he says he has Parkinson's Disease

Zoe Ward, HND Multimedia, Leeds College of art & Design, Jacob Kramer Building, Blenheim Walk, Leeds, LS2 9AG

SPONSORED BY
THE GUARDIAN

The **Guardian**

WRITING

THE BRIEF THE GUARDIAN IS SOLD AT ALL UK UNIVERSITY CAMPUS SHOPS AT THE DISCOUNTED PRICE OF 20P DURING THE WEEK. MANY STUDENTS, PARTICULARLY FIRST YEARS, ARE UNAWARE OF THE CAMPUS SHOP AND THE DISCOUNTED GUARDIAN AVAILABLE THERE. DEVELOP AN ON-CAMPUS COPY BASED AD CAMPAIGN TO ORIENTATE STUDENTS IN THE RIGHT DIRECTION.

JUDGES' COMMENTS IT IS NEVER EASY TO COMMUNICATE PRICE IN AN ENGAGING MANNER AND THAT WAS WHAT WAS NEEDED TO FORM THE HEART OF THE CREATIVE RESPONSE… AFTER SOME HEATED DEBATE THE JUDGES DECIDED THAT NEITHER WINNER SHOULD BE LAUDED ABOVE THE OTHER GIVEN THEIR VERY DIFFERENT RESPONSES TO THE BRIEF. THE FIRST IS EXTREMELY WELL CRAFTED… THE WRITING IS THE CENTREPIECE OF THE WORK AND HAS A CEREBRAL QUALITY. IN THE SECOND, STRONG WRITING SUPPORTED A ROBUST CREATIVE IDEA, AND MADE FOR A VERSATILE, CAMPAIGN ABLE SOLUTION. **KAREN BYRNE AND GILES BRENNARD**

THE BEST WORK TENDED TO BE STRIPPED DOWN AND PURELY FOCUSED ON THE WRITING. THE JOINT PRIZE-WINNERS MANAGED TO STAY VERY FOCUSED ON THE BRIEF ITSELF AND CLEVERLY WORKED THE DISCOUNT MESSAGE INTO THEIR IDEAS. A LOT HAS BEEN SAID RECENTLY ABOUT THE DEATH OF COPY IN ADVERTISING. I WAS GLAD TO FIND IT ALIVE AND DANCING TO MICHAEL JACKSON'S 'THRILLER'. **PAUL EWEN**

Karen Byrne
The Guardian

Andrew Fraser
BMP DDB

Giles Brennard
The Guardian

Paul Ewen
Saatchi & Saatchi

First

Student
Christian Stacey

Tutors
Bryn Jones
Ben Tibbs
Malcolm Kennard

College
Kingston University

First

Students
William Bingham
Victoria Daltrey

Tutors
Zelda Malan
Clive Challis
Maggie Gallagher

College
Central Saint Martins/
College of Art and Design

It's underneath the fag machine, hostage to a piece of half-chewed gum.

The Guardian
Student **Discount**
20p Monday-Friday
at the campus shop
Free Thinking. Almost.

The Guardian check here

It's buried in the sofa, next to last weeks pizza crust.

It's lodged between the carpet and the skirting board, a fugitive from the Hoover.

It's underneath the fag machine, hostage to a piece of half-chewed gum.

It's slipped beneath the passenger seat of your clapped out Fiesta.

It's at the bottom of your gym bag, suffocating in your knackered trainers.

It's under the bed, forgotten in the back pocket of your crumpled, unwashed jeans.

It's in the desk drawer, camouflaged by the paperclips.

It's lying, unclaimed, in the bottom of a vending machine.

It's 20p waiting to be found.

It's the Guardian, waiting to be read.

It's 'free thinking'. Almost.

The Guardian
The Student Discount Scheme
lets you buy the Guardian
for **20p** Monday to Friday and **60p** on Saturdays.
Find your copy at the **campus shop.**

Students
Jo Forel
Petter Lublin

Tutors
Zelda Malan
Clive Challis
Maggie Gallagher

College
Central Saint Martins/
College of Art and Design

Student
Leon Bahrani

Tutors
Bev Whitehead
Bren Nevin
Andrew Baker

College
Surrey Institute of Art and Design University College at Epsom

CUTTING A LONG STORY SHORT.

~~Pick up a copy~~ of The Guardian ~~today and receive a great offer for students. Being a bestselling newspaper, you can rely on the fact that it always~~ has ~~all up to date coverage of the very latest news, sports, arts and media. Normally a copy of the paper bought between monday and friday would have~~ been ~~50p. But, for any students at university or college, the price has been significantly and generously~~ reduced ~~so you'll receive a copy of the paper without feeling financially strained~~. To ~~take full advantage of this amazing offer which lets you have the newspaper for only~~ 20p, ~~you won't have to go far. Just drop in at your university shop/outlet which is usually situated~~ on campus.

The **Guardian**
LOWER PRICE FOR HIGHER EDUCATION

Students
Gerry Batson
Allen Bond

Tutors
Kate Bashford
Guy Preston

College
Barnet College

cut price 20p *The* **Guardian**

Students
Annette Diaz
Barbara Tejada

Tutor
Ron Seichrist

College
Miami Ad School

THE GUARDIAN

You walk out of your flat, early in the morning. Time to head to your 9:30 history class. Everyone on campus looks like they just rolled out of bed. But then you think of her. She is a vision. Always looks well rested. Her hair brushed and beautiful. Clothes are clean and pressed. How does someone look so good that early in the morning? You daydream about her as you head into class. She's the best.

There she sits. In the second row. Third seat from the right. Just like every time you walk into history class. Do you dare sit next to her today? Is today the day you make your move? Will you tell her how you feel? Not likely. You take your usual seat right behind her. You can keep your eye on her all during class.

She's so smart. Always the first to raise her hand. Always has something interesting to say. She must be the top student in the class. The other students file into the room. You glance over her shoulder to see what she is up to. She's reading a newspaper. It looks like the Guardian.

Maybe that's how she does it. You start to think about it. You've seen her reading the Guardian before. In the student lounge. At the local restaurant. That must be why she always has interesting questions. Why she always seems to know what's going on. That's how she does it.

Your mind starts to race. How do you use this to your advantage? How do you get closer to her?

Ask her where she got the Guardian. Ask her where you can get one. You will have so much to talk about. You will find things you have in common. You will go with her to the student lounge and the restaurant. You will meet up and read your Guardian's together. Like a date.

Now's your chance.

Guardian Unlimited

On sale at the campus shop. Available everyday at a discounted rate.

Students
Rob Ferrara
Liz Franklin

Tutor
Leah Klein

College
Buckinghamshire Chilterns University College

The **Guardian**

20p

only on campus

An offer so simple, even a sports science student could understand it.

CONTACT DETAILS

Academy of Art College
180 New Montgomery Street
San Francisco
CA 94105
USA
Tel   001 415 263 4185
Fax   001 415 274 2291
www.academyart.edu
Tutor
Melinda Mettler

Accademia di Communicazione
Via Savona 112/A
Milano 20144
Italy
Tel   0039 022 300 61
Fax   0039 022 300 6200
Tutor
Valentina Majocchi

Barnet College
Wood Street
Barnet
Hertfordshire EN5 4AZ
Tel   020 8440 6321
Fax   020 8441 5236
www.barnet.ac.uk
Tutors
Kate Bashford, Guy Preston

Bath Spa University College
Sion Hill
Lansdown
Bath
Avon BA1 5SF
Tel   01225 875 416
Fax   01225 875 583
Tutors
David Beaugeard, Paul Minott

Berghs School of Communication
Sveavagen 34
Box 1380
Stockholm SE-111 93
Sweden
Tel   0046 8 587 550 00
Fax   0046 8 587 550 10
www.berghs-soc.com
Tutor
William Easton

**Bergische Universitat Wuppertal
(Bugh Wuppertal)**
Haspeler Strase 27
Wuppertal 42285
Germany
Tel   0049 (0)202 439 4021
Fax   0049 (0)202 439 4188
Tutor
Hans-Gunter Schmitz

Birmingham Institute of Art and Design
Corporation Street
Gosta Green
Birmingham B4 7DX
Tel   0121 331 5830
Fax   0121 333 6020
Tutors
Kelvin Bulton, Clive Colledge, Martyn Hill,
David Knight, Paul Lander, John Lowe,
Bal Nandra, David Osbaldestin, Phil Thomson

Brunel University
Runnymead Campus
Coopers Hill Lane
Egham
Surrey TW20 0JZ
Tel   01784 431 341
Fax   01784 472 879
Tutors
Les Porter, Michelle Douglas

**Buckinghamshire Chilterns
University College**
Queen Alexandra Road
High Wycombe
Buckinghamshire HP11 2JZ
Tel   01494 522 141
Fax   01494 524 392
Tutors
Bruce Ingman, Leah Klein, Zelda Malan,
Lyndon Mallet, John Merriman,
Paul Plowman, Nigel Robinson,
Julie Wright

**Central Saint Martins/College
of Art and Design**
Southampton Row
London WC1B 4AP
Tel   020 7514 7000
Fax   020 7514 7337
www.csm.linst.ac.uk/
Tutors
Phil Baines, Ralph Ball, Cath Caldwell,
Clive Challis, Catherine Dixon, Geoff Fowle,
Maggie Gallagher, Steve Harries, Ben Hughes,
John Ingledew, Chris Lefteri, Amanda Lester,
Zelda Malan, Karla Newell, Hazel Rattigan,
Nick Rhodes, Kasia Rust, Andrew Sides,
Marc Wood, Mike Woods

Chelsea College of Art and Design
Manresa Road
London SW3 6LS
Tel   020 7514 7750
Tutor
Geoffrey Thomas-Shaw

Curtin University
Kent Street
Bentley 6102
Australia
Tel   0061 9266 7611
Fax   0061 9266 2711
Tutor
Blair McLeish

De Montfort University
Fletcher Building
The Gateway
Leicester LE1 9BH
Tel   01162 551 551
Fax   01162 577 574
www.dmu.ac.uk
Tutor
Chris Hinton

Doncaster College
Church View
Waterdale
Doncaster
South Yorkshire DN1 3EX
Tel   01302 553 553
Fax   01302 553 838
Tutors
David Bullers, Simon Gomes

Duncan of Jordanstone College of Art
Perth Road
Dundee DD1 4HT
Tel   01382 223 261
Fax   01382 201 378
Tutors
David Herbert, Gordon Robertson

Dunstable College
Kingsway
Dunstable
Bedfordshire LU5 4HG
Tel   01582 477 776
Fax   01582 478 801
www.dunstable.ac.uk
Tutors
Malcolm Jobling, Nick Jeeves

Ecole Cantonale D'Art de Lausanne
4 Avenue de L'Elysee
Lausanne 1006
Switzerland
Tel   0041 21 316 9220
Fax   0041 21 316 9266
luc.bergerton@dfj.vd.ch
Tutors
Remy Jacquet, Patrick Reymond

Edinburgh College of Art
Lauriston Place
Edinburgh
Leith EH3 9DF
Tel   0131 229 9311
Fax   0131 221 6001
www.eca.ac.uk
Tutor
Zoë Patterson

Edinburgh's Telford College
North Campus
Edinburgh
Leith EH4 2NZ
Tel   0131 332 2491
Tutors
Jan Fitzpatrick, Brian Shaw

Fachhochschule Mainz
Fachrichtung Design
Seppl-Gluckert Passage 10
Mainz D-55116
Germany
Tel   0049 69 63 74 352
Fax   0049 69 92 31 8033
Tutors
Thomas Daum, Charlotte Schroner

Falmouth College of Arts
Wood Lane
Falmouth
Cornwall TR11 4RA
Tel   01326 211 077
Fax   01326 213 809
www.falmouth.ac.uk
Tutors
Alice Kavounas Taylor, Digby Atkinson

**Forsbergs School of Graphic
Design and Advertising**
Polhemsgatan 29
Box 8173
Stockholm 10420
Sweden
Tel   0046 8 652 3940
Fax   0046 8 654 7510
Tutors
Peter Viksten, Dennis Dahlqvist

Glasgow College of Building and Printing
60 North Hanover Street
Glasgow
Strathclyde G1 2BP
Tel   0141 332 9969
Tutors
Joanna Caskey, Liliana Rodriguez, Keith Moir

**Hastings College of Arts and
Technology in affiliation with
The University of Brighton**
Archery Road
St Leonards-on-Sea
East Sussex TN38 OHX
Tel   01424 442 222
Fax   01424 721 763
Tutors
Andrew Aloof, David Fowler

**Hong Kong Institute of
Vocational Education**
Rm 319, 21 Yuen Wo Road
Shatin, Hong Kong
China
Tel   00852 2256 7438
Fax   00852 2256 7477
Tutors
Sannia Ho, Simon Wang

Instituto Politecnico do Porto
Rua D. Sancho 1
981 4480-771
Vila do Conde
Portugal
Tutor
Steve Sarson

Kingston University
Knights Park
Kingston upon Thames
Surrey KT1 2QJ
Tel   020 8547 2000
www.kingston.ac.uk
Tutors
Bryn Jones, Malcolm Kennard, Brian Love,
Ben Tibbs

Leeds College of Art and Design
The Jacob Kramer Building
Blenheim Walk
Leeds
Yorkshire LS2 9AQ
Tel   0113 202 8000
Fax   0113 244 5916
www.leeds-art.ac.uk
Tutor
Course Team

London College of Printing
Elephant & Castle
London SE1 6SB
Tel   020 7514 6500
Fax   020 7514 6674
Tutors
Dominic Dyson, Alan Sekers

Loughborough University
Loughborough
Leicestershire LE11 3TU
Tel   01509 261 515
Fax   01509 265 515
Tutors
Anne Colwell, Mike Davidson,
Mario Minichiello

Miami Ad School
955 Alton Road
Miami Beach
Florida 33139
USA
Tel   001 305 538 3193
Fax   001 305 538 3724
Tutors
Karen Birnholz, Tom Lunt, Ron Seichrist,
Jerry Torchia, Renetta Welty

Middlesex University
Cat Hill
Barnet
Hertfordshire EN4 8HT
Tel   020 8362 5000
Fax   020 8362 5159
Tutors
Geoff Grandfield, Andrew Grossett,
Geoff Haddon, Phil Healey,
Lilian Lindblom-Smith, Robert Shadbolt,
Nancy Slonims

Napier University
School of Design and Media Arts
Merchiston Campus
10 Colinton Road
Edinburgh
Leith EH10 5DT
Tel 0131 444 2266
Tutors
Andrew Gliddens, Ian Lambert, Alex Milton,
Isla Munro, Paul Rodgers, Bjorn Rodnes,
Will Titley

Newcastle Under Lyme College
Trinity Building
Liverpool Road
Newcastle Under Lyme
Staffordshire ST5 2DF
Tutors
Mike Kelly, Ron Mitchelll

North Wales School of Art and Design
Plas Coch Mold Road
Wrexham LL11 2AW
Tel 01978 290 666
Fax 01978 310 060
www.newi.ac.uk/nwsad
Tutors
David Gill, Andy Holt, Alan Summers

**Ravensbourne College of
Design and Communication**
3-D Design
Walden Road
Chislehurst
Kent BR7 5SN
Tel 020 8289 4900
Tutors
Sian Cook, John Durrant, Andrew McRae,
Martin Schooley

School for Commercial Communication
W.G. Plein 332
Amsterdam 1054 SG
Netherlands
Tel 0031 20 489 8727
Fax 0031 35 215 391
Tutors
Dave Morris, Marien de Goffau

Sheffield Hallam University
School of Cultural Studies
Psalter Lane
Sheffield
Yorkshire S11 8UZ
Tel 0114 225 5555
www.shu.ac.uk
Tutors
Glyn Hawley, Claire Lockwood, Bill Stewart

Somerset College of Art and Technology
Wellington Road
Taunton
Somerset TA1 5AX
Tel 01823 366 366
www.somerset.ac.uk
Tutors
Guy Lawrence, Widge Hunt,
Malcolm Swatridge

Southampton Institute
Media Arts Faculty
East Park Terrace
Southampton
Hampshire S014 0RD
Tel 023 8031 9000
Fax 023 8031 9227
www.solent.ac.uk
Tutors
Kate Bonella, David Gardener, Vicky Isley,
Paul Shakespeare, Paul Smith

Southwark College
Surrey Docks Centre
Drummond Road
London SE16 4EE
Tel 020 7815 1500
Tutors
Derek Yates, Elliot Thoburn, Charlotte Oelerich

**Surrey Institute of Art and Design
University College at Epsom**
Ashley Road
Epsom
Surrey KT18 5BE
Tel 01372 728 811
Fax 01372 747 050
Tutors
Andrew Baker, Robert De Niet, Bren Nevin,
Calum Mackenzie, Andrea Taylor,
Bev Whitehead

Swindon College
Regents Circus
Swindon
Wiltshire SN1 1PT
Tel 01793 491 591
Fax 01793 641 794
Tutors
Peter Benson, Greg Rendell

Temasek Polytechnic
21 Tampines Avenue
529757 Singapore
Tel 0065 780 5720
Fax 0065 784 6144
Tutor
Irwanta Salim

The Arts Institute Bournemouth
Wallisdown Road
Poole
Dorset BH12 5HH
Tel 01202 533 011
Fax 01202 537 729
www.aid.ac.uk
Tutor
Roger Gould

The Creative Circus
812 Lambert Drive, N.E.
Atlanta
Georgia 30324
USA
Tel 001 404 607 8880
Fax 001 404 875 1590
Tutors
Norm Grey, Mike Weed

The School Agency
Santa Leonor
61 1Nave 2
Madrid 28037
Spain
Tel 0034 1 754 03 75
Fax 0034 1 754 07 75
Tutors
Jose Maria de Armas, Chus Isidro,
Florencia Montes, Marcelo Montes

University College Northampton
Avenue Campus
St George's Avenue
Northampton
Northamptonshire NN2 6JD
Tel 01604 735 500
Fax 01604 717 813
www.northampton.ac.uk
Tutors
John Holt, Ian Newsham, Barry Wenden,
Paul Wilson

University of Central England
Linden Road
Bournville
Birmingham B30 1JX
Tel 0121 331 5762
Tutor
Kevin Harley

Lasalle-Sia College of the Arts
90 Goodman Road
439053 Singapore
Tel 0065 6340 9172
Fax 0065 6345 7475
Tutor
Patricia Campbell

University of Central Lancashire
Victoria Building
Victoria Street
Preston
Lancashire PR1 2HE
Tel 01772 893 372
Fax 01772 892 920
www.uclan.ac.uk
Tutors
Andy Bainbridge, Ron Bray, Mark Lamey,
Mike Moran, Tom Shaughnessy, Lin Sinclair,
Jane Souyave, Pete Thompson

University of Glamorgan
Treforest
Pontypridd
Mid Glamorgan CF37 1DL
Tel 01443 480480
glam.ac.uk
Tutors
Judith Hills, Gerald Emanuel

University of Gloucestershire
Pitville Campus
Albert Road
Cheltenham
Gloucestershire GL52 2JG
Tel 01242 532 210
Fax 01242 532 207
www.glos.ac.uk
Tutors
Frank Holmes, Jon Dytor, Nick Holmes,
Dave Sturdy

University of Hertfordshire
College Lane
Hatfield
Hertfordshire AL10 9AB
Tel 01707 284 000
Fax 01707 284 115
Tutors
Michael Goatman, Julian Lindley

University of Lincoln
Queens Gardens
Kingston upon Hull HU1 3DQ
Tel 01482 440 550
Fax 01482 462 101
Tutor
Alan Thomas

University of Lincoln
Thomas Parker House
13/14 Silver Street
Lincoln LN2 1HJ
Tel 01522 895 211
Fax 01522 895 244
Tutors
Chris Dune, Phil Eastwood, Carolyn Puzzovio,
Barrie Tullett, Phillipa Wood

University of Northumbria at Newcastle
School of Design
Squires Building
Sandyford Road
Newcastle NE1 8ST
Tel 0191 227 4913
Fax 0191 227 4655
www.unn.ac.uk
Tutors
Steve Burdett, Debbie Douglas

University of Portsmouth
Eldon Building
Winston Churchill Avenue
Portsmouth
Hampshire PO1 2DJ
Tel 023 9287 6543
Tutors
Simon Clarke, Joachim Hetzel, Jon Hares

University of Westminster
Warwick Road
Harrow
Middlesex HA1 3TP
Tel 020 7911 5000
Fax 020 7911 5943
Tutor
Christine McCauley

VCU Adcenter
1313 East Main Street
Richmond
Virginia 23219
USA
Tel 001 804 828 8384
Fax 001 804 828 4210
Tutors
Mark Fensky, Coz Cotzias, Pat Burnham,
Charlie Kouns

West Thames College
PO Box 225
London Road
Isleworth
Middlesex TW7 4HS
Tel 020 8326 2000
Fax 020 8326 2266/2001
www.west-thames.ac.uk
Tutors
Richard Haydon, Mike Comley

SUMMARY OF WINNING COLLEGES

College	Nominations for Prizes	Work in Annual	Page Number(s)
Academy of Art College		1	137
Accademia di Communicazione	2 (1)	3 (3)	27, 52-53
Barnet College	1	2 (1)	36, 182
Bath Spa University College	4	4 (3)	25, 56-57, 134
Berghs School of Communication		1	46
Bergische Universitat Wuppertal		1	99
Birmingham Institute of Art and Design	2	4	32, 99, 121, 164
Brunel University	1	1	97
Buckinghamshire Chilterns University College	8 (11)	18 (21)	27, 30-32, 66, 68, 70-71, 80, 102, 124, 140-143, 145, 151, 166, 183
Central Saint Martins/College of Art and Design	11 (11)	21 (19)	13, 24, 37, 39, 67-69, 71, 98, 113-114, 116-117, 122-125, 165, 168-169, 179-180
Chelsea College of Art and Design	2 (1)	3 (2)	78, 124, 154-155
Curtin University	1	1	75
De Montfort University		1	159
Doncaster College	1	1	17
Duncan of Jordanstone College of Art	3 (5)	3 (9)	96, 157-158
Dunstable College	1	2	45, 165
Ecole Cantonale D'Art de Lausanne	4 (4)	4 (6)	60-61, 112
Edinburgh College of Art		2 (1)	166, 168
Edinburgh's Telford College		1	20
Fachhochschule Mainz	2 (1)	4 (1)	106-108
Falmouth College of Arts		1	38
Forsbergs School of Graphic Design and Advertising	(1)	1 (1)	92
Glasgow College of Building and Printing		1 (1)	63
Hastings College of Arts and Technology	1	1 (1)	58
Hong Kong Institute of Vocational Education		1	40
Instituto Politecnico do Porto		1	131
Kingston University	2 (5)	3 (8)	8-9, 93, 178
Lasalle-Sia College of the Arts		1	59
Leeds College of Art and Design	1 (1)	3 (3)	148, 151, 158
London College of Printing	1 (1)	2 (1)	128, 131
Loughborough University	(1)	2 (1)	109, 174
Miami Ad School	2	6 (1)	31, 39, 69, 130, 135, 183
Middlesex University	3 (1)	6 (4)	16, 70, 84, 90, 93, 166
Napier University	2 (3)	4 (7)	62, 81, 115, 117
Newcastle Under Lyme College	1	1	74
North Wales School of Art and Design	1	1 (1)	156
Ravensbourne College of Design and Communication	1 (3)	2 (4)	103, 108
School for Commercial Communication		1	20
Sheffield Hallam University	2 (1)	5 (2)	53-55, 59, 62
Somerset College of Art and Technology	2	3	18, 26, 44
Southampton Institute	2 (1)	4 (3)	103, 151, 165, 175
Southwark College	1	2	91, 120
Surrey Institute of Art and Design University College at Epsom	2 (1)	4 (6)	38, 92, 150, 181
Swindon College		2 (1)	136, 159
Temasek Polytechnic	1 (1)	1 (1)	172
The Arts Institute Bournemouth		2	49, 167
The Creative Circus		2 (1)	40, 130
The School Agency	1	3	19, 134
University College Northampton	2	2 (2)	85, 173
University of Central England	(4)	1 (9)	122
University of Central Lancashire	4 (1)	11 (4)	19, 21, 41, 86-87, 129-130, 135, 143
University of Glamorgan	1	2	46, 115
University of Gloucestershire		3 (1)	18, 75, 144
University of Hertfordshire	1	1	112
University of Lincoln	1 (1)	5 (2)	47-48, 149-150, 174
University of Northumbria at Newcastle	(2)	2	47-48
University of Portsmouth	1	1 (4)	79
University of Westminster		1 (1)	91
VCU Adcenter	(1)	2 (2)	12, 131
West Thames College		1	33
Total	**79**	**176**	

Figures in brackets denote last year's figures.

INDEX OF STUDENTS

A
Rihwa Ahn	128
John Aitchison	31
Esther Alcaide	36
Ottilia Aviram	91

B
Daniel Baer	122
Leon Bahrani	181
Harinder Bajwa	129
Paul Bakker	20
Lisa Balm	18
Jesper Bange	69
Adam Bates	97
Gerry Batson	182
Chris Baxter	158
Richard Baxter	103
Melissa Bell	137
Richard Bell	166
Scott Bell	135
Andrew Bellamy	167
Paul-Michael Berwise-Ebanks	120
Daniel Bessex	115
Kerry Bilton	17
William Bingham	13, 179
James Birchall	143
Leon Bonaventura	150
Allen Bond	182
Charlotte Bond	18
Tracey Brassington	57
Alex Braxton	24
Christen Brestrup	143
Anna Ines Briano	19
Paul Brink	69
Pauline Bucher	61
Christine Buhl	107
Christopher Butler	156

C
Caterina Calabro	27
Victoria Callister	129
Nicole Chamberlain	150
Taikee Chan	84
Nolan Chandler	112
Lee Choo Chin	16
Alison Ching	123
Gareth Chubb	46
Kim Clark	45
Lesley Coleman	130
Ben Cox	44
Maria Crompton	19

D
Rochus Dahnken	108
Victoria Daltrey	13, 179
Tushar Date	31
Ray Dauncey	151
Emma Davey	32
Matthew Davies	47
Hayley Davis	144
Chris Day	18

D
Belen De Azcarate	19
Isabel Octavio De Toledo	134
Stella Deacon	70
Nick Dell'anno	38
Kim Devall	130
Annette Diaz	183
Rick Dodds	32
Alan Dowds	63
Michael Duncan	136
Sarah Dutton	21

E
Cheynne Edmonston	90
Jon Eley	166
Justin Elliot	174
Julia Elton-Bott	75
Catherine Etchells	75
Chris Evans	151
Sam Evans	175

F
Rodrigo Fernandes	39
Rob Ferrara	68, 140, 183
Stephen Flynn	157
Keeley Foord	58
Jo Forel	67, 180
Liz Franklin	68, 140, 183
Mikael Friden	122

G
Tamsin Garbutt	19
Lindsay Gill	144
Jonathan Goodall	148
Vanessa Gorman	151
Nicole Gotti	61
Julia Greiner	106
Julia Greisbach	124
Alex Griffin	49
Ekaterina Grizik	106
Csilla Gyertyanosi	107

H
Kathrina Hahn	30
Louise Halliwell	21
Emily Hancock	54
Jennifer Handline	135
Joe Harries	37
Sarah Harris	27
Charlotte Hayes	56
Scott Hayes	40
Hao He	55
Vicki Heath	143
Iain Hector	165
Sebastian Heilig	108
Till Heim	108
Rebecca Hembrow	66
Georgina Hewitt	166
Anna Hjertqvist	165
Eva Hoefer	107

H
Claire Holden	20
Stephen Howell	30
James Hughes	122
Emma Hunt	123
Craig Hunter	151

I
Giulia Inaudi	53
Grey Ingram	12, 131
Tomoko Ishii	98
Maya Ishizaki	113

J
Lany Jaros	130
Ryan Joiner	168
Tanja Jonath-Pieoler	107

K
Mahab Kazmi	68
Sebastiaan Kenter	20
Paul Kinsella	41, 130, 135
Kevin Koller	31
Nikolai Kolstad	68
Wei Yee Kung	70

L
Sam Lachlan	56, 134
Vicki Lau	91
Pie Lee-Mun	164
Joshua Leigh	169
David Leisinger Zhirong	172
Karry Leung	71
Wai Yuen Leung	40
Emma Lewis	18
Daniel Liden	114
Yi Lin Lin	131
Mattias Lindstedt	46
Brad Logan	48
Rodrigo Lopez Caruana	19
Petter Lublin	67, 180
Asa Lucander	93
Sam Luk	87
Helen Lumby	71
Rhavin Lutchman	38

M
Hew Fuen Ma	151
Lawrence Mann	158
Teresa Marcos Franco	19
Nicolas Markwald	99
Sarah McCauley	116
Kelly McDonald	143
Debbie McKay	96
Joss McKinley	125
Roderick McLachlan	81
Anna McManus	115
Ben Middleton	141-142
Lisa Mitchell	32

M
Andrea Mineo	27
Morton Moerland	92
Azza Mohamed Suliman	121
Philippa Morrice	39

N
Rosie Neave	148
Nina Neusitzer	99
Simon Newman	74
Clive Nicholson	93
Catherine Nippe	79
Alberto Noda	19
Martin Norrlind	92

O
Christian Osmers	137
Linus Ostberg	92
Stuart Outhwaite	141-142

P
Basia Paczesna	123
Anna Palama	27
Joo Young Park	55
Adam Parker	70
Byron Parr	168
Imran Patel	145
Gemma Pearce	75
David Peasland	166
Diego Perez	134
Danny Perrett	165
Dave Prater	145
Alan Pride	62
George Primentas	131

R
Rebecca Raftery	66
Simon Ramsay	158
Yvonne Reuter	106
Pete Richardson	129
James Roadley-Battin	159
Joseph Roberts	149
Paul Roberts	47
Tom Robinson	103
Jorge Miguel Rodrigo Blanco	19
Gina Rossi	69
Stephan Roux	80
Adrien Rovero	112
Tom Rowley	102
John Russel	63
David Ryan	33

S
Patricia Saavedra	53
Jamie Sage	78
Eric Schmitt	107
Robert Schwartz	108
Ben Scott	33
Alex Shapowal	117

S
Keshni Sharma	123
Ooi Shur Ling	59
Nina Sletten	99
Charlotte Smalley	71
Daniel Smith	62
Tom Smith	173
Tim Smyllie	154
Christian Stacey	8-9, 178
Ed Stanton	117
Lisa Sternberg	130
Tom Stimpson	48
Guenaelle Stulz	60

T
Bruno Tavares	131
Barbara Tejada	130, 183
Will Thacker	38
Laura Thomson	63
Maari Thrall	40
Hannah Tourle	26
Lisa Tse	116
Natalie Turner	59

V
Chi Van Nim	91
Jose Luis Varon Garces	134
Bies Vermeulen	20
Pasquale Volpe	52
Gregor Von Sievers	107

W
Mark Ward	24
Robert Ward	21
Neil Watts	85
Derrick Webb	12, 131
Klaire Webster	109
Greg Wharton	86
Edward Whatton	159
Paul Whidbourne	124
Gary Williams	27
Jason Williams	174
Karen Williamson	75
Cynthia Wong	41, 130, 135
Tim Wood	38

Y
Claire Yates	25

D&AD STUDENT AWARDS SCHEME

ELIGIBILITY ALL FULL-TIME STUDENTS STUDYING AT UNIVERSITIES, COLLEGES AND ART SCHOOLS IN THE UK, EUROPE AND OVERSEAS ARE ELIGIBLE TO ENTER THE COMPETITION, EITHER AS INDIVIDUALS OR AS TEAMS OF UP TO THREE (E.G. DESIGNER, PHOTOGRAPHER, COPYWRITER). BRIEFS ARE SET AND MUST BE COMPLETED IN THE ENGLISH LANGUAGE.

ELIGIBILITY MAY VARY SLIGHTLY FOR ADDITIONAL SCHEMES FALLING UNDER THE MAIN STUDENT AWARDS PROGRAMME, SUCH AS THE WPP BURSARIES AND NESTA PRODUCT DESIGN AND INNOVATION AWARDS. PLEASE CONTACT THE EDUCATION DEPARTMENT AT D&AD FOR FURTHER INFORMATION.

JUDGING THE JUDGING TAKES PLACE IN APRIL. THERE ARE TWO ROUNDS OF JUDGING, THE FIRST TO DETERMINE WHICH WORK WILL BE FEATURED IN THE STUDENT ANNUAL, AND THE SECOND TO CHOOSE, FROM THIS SELECTION, FIRST AND SECOND PRIZE-WINNERS AND COMMENDATIONS.

EACH CATEGORY IS VIEWED BY ITS OWN PANEL WHICH CONSISTS OF THE SPONSORS AND WRITERS OF THE BRIEF, AND SENIOR CREATIVES FROM RENOWNED AND APPROPRIATE AGENCIES AND STUDIOS.

ANNOUNCEMENT OF WINNERS THE RESULTS ARE ANNOUNCED AT THE STUDENT AWARDS CEREMONY IN JULY. ALL SELECTED WORK IS PUBLISHED IN THE STUDENT ANNUAL. THE STUDENT WORK THAT HAS BEEN NOMINATED FOR AN AWARD IS EXHIBITED AT THE PRESENTATION NIGHT AND ALSO AT NEW BLOOD, HELD IN LONDON IN THE LAST WEEK OF JUNE. THE WORK IS ALSO SHOWCASED ON THE D&AD BLOODBANK WEBSITE, WITH FIRST AND SECOND PRIZE WINNERS BEING PUBLISHED IN THE D&AD PROFESSIONAL AWARDS ANNUAL.

AWARDS CEREMONY PRIZES ARE PRESENTED AT THE AWARDS CEREMONY IN FRONT OF AN AUDIENCE MADE UP OF JUDGES, SPONSORS, D&AD'S EDUCATION COUNCIL, TUTORS AND STUDENTS.

AWARDS AND PRIZES FIRST AND SECOND PRIZE WINNERS RECEIVE A YELLOW PENCIL, SPECIALLY DESIGNED FOR THE STUDENT AWARDS. THERE ARE ALSO CASH PRIZES FOR FIRST (£1,000), SECOND (£400) AND COMMENDED (£250) PRIZE WINNERS IN EACH CATEGORY. AN ADDITIONAL CASH PRIZE OF £1,000 FOR STUDENT OF THE YEAR IS AWARDED FOR BEST OVERALL SUBMISSION. PRIZE MONEY IN 2003 TOTALLED £46,000. CERTIFICATES ARE AWARDED TO STUDENTS AND TUTORS FOR ALL WORK RECEIVING AN AWARD. IN ADDITION, ALL FIRST AND SECOND PRIZE WINNERS ARE INVITED TO BECOME NEW BLOOD MEMBERS OF D&AD FOR ONE YEAR, FREE OF CHARGE. AS NEW BLOOD MEMBERS THEY RECEIVE COPIES OF AMPERSAND – D&AD'S QUARTERLY NEWSLETTER, DISCOUNTED TICKETS TO THE PRESIDENT'S LECTURES AS WELL AS OTHER BENEFITS AND OCCASIONAL SPECIAL OFFERS.

2004 AWARDS TIMETABLE

OCTOBER 2003 CALL FOR ENTRIES MAILED

MARCH 2004 ENTRY DEADLINE

WWW.DANDAD.ORG/BLOODBANK

Try having your own ideas.

workout Twenty three sessions designed to help professionals think outside the book. Do something inspired today, contact Laura Woodroffe on +44 (0)20 7840 1126 or laura@dandad.co.uk. It could be your way in.

www.dandad.org

ACKNOWLEDGEMENTS
PROJECT DEVELOPED AND
COORDINATED BY D&AD
(BRITISH DESIGN & ART DIRECTION)

CLAIRE FENNELOW
EDUCATION AND TRAINING DIRECTOR

JO MAUDE
ACTING EDUCATION DIRECTOR

IAN WILLINGHAM
STUDENT AWARDS MANAGER

ANNA BAILEY
COLLEGE PROGRAMME MANAGER

CHRIS THOMPSON
COLLEGE AND GRADUATE PROGRAMME MANAGER

LAURA WOODROFFE
TRAINING PROGRAMME MANAGER

NIA EVANS
EDUCATION OFFICER

AMI NIELSON
DEVELOPMENT DIRECTOR

CAROLINE DOUGHTY
SPONSORSHIP MANAGER

EMILY WHEELER
DEVELOPMENT MANAGER

VICKY ELTRINGHAM
DEVELOPMENT OFFICER

AWARDS TEAM
ROBERT WHEELER
STEPHANIE TETT
NICK LYNCH
SARAH GROOM
TAHITA BULMER

CAMPAIGN AND ANNUAL DESIGNED BY BROWNS/LONDON

BACK COVER/ENDPAPER PHOTOGRAPHY BY DAVY JONES

JURY PHOTOGRAPHY BY CHRISTINE DONNIER-VALENTIN

WORK PHOTOGRAPHY BY THE PACKSHOT FACTORY

TYPESETTING BY SAFFRON DIGITAL PRODUCTION

ANNUAL PRINTED BY VENTURA WORKS!

COVER AND ENDPAPERS: CHALLENGER OFFSET 140GSM TEXT: HANNOART SILK 150GSM SUPPLIED BY MCNAUGHTON PAPER MANUFACTURED BY SAPPI

FAX BACK
THE IDEA FOR THIS YEAR'S STUDENT AWARDS PRINT CAMPAIGN WAS TO GIVE STUDENTS WORLDWIDE THE OPPORTUNITY TO HAVE THEIR IDEAS FEATURED IN THE ANNUAL. FOUR QUESTIONS WERE POSED (SHOWN OPPOSITE THE CONTENTS) AND THE MOST INTERESTING/CREATIVE REPLIES HAVE APPEARED ON THE CATEGORY DIVIDER PAGES IN THIS ANNUAL AND IN A FEW OTHER PLACES. FROM THE HUNDREDS OF FAXES RECEIVED 30 WERE CHOSEN FOR THE CAMPAIGN, LISTED AS FOLLOWS:

FC STEVE PARK, PAUL WILSON, PAUL LEE, GRAHAM WALKER AND SADIQ RAHMAN
BLACKPOOL AND THE FYLDE COLLEGE

006 GAIL LINGARD
GLASGOW SCHOOL OF ART

010 ANDY BAINBRIDGE
UNIVERSITY OF CENTRAL LANCASHIRE

014 GARETH THOMAS
SOUTHAMPTON UNIVERSITY

022 COLETTE MCMENEMY
GLASGOW SCHOOL OF ART

028 ROB ELLIS AND NICK HORNE
BUCKINGHAMSHIRE CHILTERNS UNIVERSITY COLLEGE

034 STEVEN CROUCH
KENT INSTITUTE OF ART AND DESIGN

042 RANALD GRAHAM
GLASGOW SCHOOL OF ART

050 SARAH LONGWORTH
EDINBURGH COLLEGE OF ART

064 EILIDH MCDONALD
EDINBURGH COLLEGE OF ART

072 JAMIE YOUNG
GLASGOW SCHOOL OF ART

076 GEORGE HADLEY
KINGSTON UNIVERSITY

082 NICK MEAKINS
OXFORD COLLEGE OF FURTHER EDUCATION

088 JOHN NIELSEN
SOUTH CHESHIRE COLLEGE

094 LINDSEY BUCHANAN
GLASGOW SCHOOL OF ART

100 CHRIS JAMES
KINGSTON UNIVERSITY

104 RANALD GRAHAM
GLASGOW SCHOOL OF ART

110 MATTHEW HART
KENT INSTITUTE OF ART AND DESIGN

118 CARLY MCGOVERN
EDINBURGH COLLEGE OF ART

126 HUGH JANUS?
UNIVERSITY OF EAST LONDON

132 JAMES GREG
GLASGOW SCHOOL OF ART

138 SONO SUZUKI
EDINBURGH COLLEGE OF ART

146 RICHARD NEWELL
AND PETE WILLIAMS
UNIVERSITY OF GLOUCESTERSHIRE

152 MICHAEL SIMPSON
SURREY INSTITUTE OF ART AND DESIGN

160 PRIYA REKHI
EDINBURGH COLLEGE OF ART

162 STEVE PARK, PAUL WILSON, PAUL LEE
GRAHAM WALKER AND SADIQ RAHMAN
BLACKPOOL AND THE FYLDE COLLEGE

170 TRUDE HANSEN
BUSKERUD UNIVERSITY COLLEGE
NORWAY

176 ZOE WARD
LEEDS COLLEGE OF ART AND DESIGN

CEREMONY INVITE
FRASER CROALL
EDINBURGH COLLEGE OF ART

ORDER OF CEREMONY
GRUFFYDD MORGAN
KINGSTON UNIVERSITY

D&AD
9 GRAPHITE SQUARE
VAUXHALL WALK
LONDON SE11 5EE
TEL +44 (0) 20 7840 1111
WWW.DANDAD.ORG
INFO@DANDAD.CO.UK

CHARITY NUMBER 305992

COPYRIGHT 2003
BRITISH DESIGN & ART DIRECTION

PUBLISHED BY D&AD

ALL RIGHTS RESERVED

UNDER NO CIRCUMSTANCES
CAN ANY PART OF THIS BOOK BE
REPRODUCED OR COPIED IN ANY
FORM, WITHOUT PRIOR PERMISSION
OF THE COPYRIGHT OWNERS.

CAN YOU DRAW A FERRET? FAX +44 (0)20 7407 9075 BEST RESPONSES PRINTED IN THE D&AD STUDENT AWARDS ANNUAL 2003 WWW.DANDAD.ORG

CAN YOU

WHAT IS IT YOU REALLY WANT?

YES! I CAN DRAW A FERRET

NO!

A FERRET?

WORLD PEACE AND PRADA